The
Mutual Fund
Wealth Builder

THE MUTUAL FUND WEALTH BUILDER

A Mutual Fund Strategy
That Won't Let You Down
No Matter What the
Market Is Doing

Michael D. Hirsch

HarperBusiness
A Division of HarperCollinsPublishers

The Library of Congress has catalogued the hardcover edition as follows:

Hirsch, Michael D.
    The mutual fund wealth builder: a mutual fund strategy that won't let you down no matter what the market is doing/ Michael D. Hirsch.
      p. cm.
    Includes index.
    ISBN 0-88730-482-6
    1. Mutual funds.   I. Title.
    HG4530.H573   1991   91-25991
    332.63'27—dc20

ISBN 0-88730-576-8 (pbk.)

92 93 94 95 96 CW 10 9 8 7 6 5 4 3 2 1

To
Terry Ronald,
a true fighter

CONTENTS

PREFACE

Let me begin with an admission. Sixteen and a half years ago, in January 1975, to be specific, I pioneered the investment approach detailed in this book. After the calamity that had befallen go-go funds earlier in that decade, building a new approach around the use of mutual funds might have seemed foolhardy, but I was convinced it would work.

And work it did. Year after year after year. Below average performance in up markets, above-average in flat markets, superior in down markets. An unbroken string of positive annual returns was being amassed, refinements were added, and the concept took hold.

But there was a problem. I knew this approach worked, but I didn't know *why*. Why did this portfolio of funds technique work so well in providing safe, consistent returns? Why could every bullet be dodged with virtual equanimity? I like to subject myself to periodic introspection—what I'm doing right, what I'm doing wrong, what can and needs to be improved, etc. For all the time spent on examining this unique investment style, however, I could never come up with the *why*.

Not even as I wrote my first book on the subject, *Multi-fund Investing*, in 1985–1986, did I have the handle.

Not until 1989. By then, I was being called upon with some regularity to explain the concept to various groups of investors, financial planners, brokers, and bankers. This one time I was in the conference room of an estate planning firm in New Jersey about to begin my presentation, when I decided to take a slightly different track. Being a strong proponent of the KISS principle (Keep It Simple, Stupid) particularly as it pertains to investment matters, I thought, "Why not go through some basic math with these people to show the benefits of this approach?"

Pop! The proverbial light bulb went on in my head. With Magic Marker in hand and easel in front of me, I began furiously scribbling out the mathematics detailed later in this book: how losses have a greater impact on long-term results than gains; how the gains required to offset losses multiply almost geometrically the larger the losses get; how you never need especially large gains in any single year to achieve good long-term results as long as you are always linking gains—the power of compounding.

I was overjoyed. I finally had the answer to why it works. I had designed an investment style which sought to limit losses rather than maximize gains, and that in itself explains why other investment theories—matching, portfolio insurance, etc.—come and go, and this one continues to work (the proud papa is happy to report that it is now in the middle of its seventeenth consecutive year of achieving positive returns). Losses have a greater impact on the portfolio than gains. Period!

But as they say, there is nothing new under the sun. As I began to pen this manuscript with its overriding theme of how to win by not losing, I discovered that the venerable Adam Smith is quoted as saying something to the effect of "The road to winning begins by not losing." And the subtitle of a recent treatise on investment policy by one of the most insightful observers of the investment scene today, Charles Ellis, is subtitled "Winning the Losers' Game." So much for original thought! (Since we live in a litigious society let me admit shamefacedly, but to protect myself from claims of plagiarism, that I have not had the occasion to read either text cited above.)

One final thought. It struck me many times while writing

this book that I was truly asking a great deal of the reader. In our daily life we are bombarded constantly by positive assaults on our psyche. Marketers sell benefits (positives); Madison Avenue allows only positive messages to come through their ads; Wall Street hypes upside potential. I recall an old 78 my sisters played on our Victrola when I was a young boy, "You have to ac-cent-uate the positive." Upside, upside, that's all we hear about.

And now comes the heretic Hirsch and asks you to put all that aside. Forget positives, forget upside. Focus solely on limiting the downside. Don't worry about how your portfolio performs during bull markets; it's almost immaterial. Focus solely on the downside. I know that's quite a leap of faith to ask of anyone brought up in the traditional investment manner, but trust me, by the time you finish reading this book you will, I hope, have come around to my way of thinking.

I am also asking the reader to put aside the ingrained notion most of us have that investing should be exciting. Wrong. Investing should be boring. As boring as watching a tortoise race against a hare (more on tortoise funds later). As boring as picking up your passbook savings account once every three months and seeing that your total has grown one to two percent. Another leap of faith: Investing is B-O-R-I-N-G.

And, as if that weren't enough, I am also asking the reader to give up bragging rights. You know: "My stocks are up ——% this year (the number in the blank is always a multiple of what the general market is doing). How are yours doing?" Sorry, but your portfolio from now on will lag when markets are rising. And unless you have a sadistic streak, I doubt you will feel comfortable gloating over how little you've lost while others have suffered major financial setbacks.

So, I admit I am asking a great deal from you. But as they say, the proof is in the pudding. If you will be satisfied with safe, consistent returns, never again having to stand by and watch your portfolio go into the tank for 20–30 percent, and having a much higher degree of assurance than you ever had in the past of hitting your target, then this book is for you. The approach is tried and tested and has worked faultlessly for seventeen years. Enjoy!

ACKNOWLEDGMENTS

I could not have been a good husband, father, and boss while writing this book without the complete and unwavering support of my family and staff. So, first of all, thank you to my wife, Jane, and to Jill, Joseph, Daniel, Marc, and Michael B. To the investment team (past and present)—Joelle, Mary, Daniel, Robin, Ann, Janet, Michelle, Glenn, Joe, Mimi, Charles, Sandy, Anne, and Andrea,—thanks for the assistance and understanding.

To my editors at Harper, particularly Martha and Susan, thanks for keeping the great procrastinator on schedule (I hit almost all my deadlines).

Much of the tabular information throughout the book credits the source, but special thanks to Bob Levy and his associates at CDA Investment Technologies, Mike Lipper and his team at Lipper Analytical, and Steve Leuthold (Northwest's favorite passenger) and all those at The Leuthold Group who have made our job as managers of mutual fund portfolios that much easier.

For the past ten years I have enjoyed a working relationship with perhaps the most soundly run bank in the United States—Republic National Bank of New York. To the senior officials of that organization—Edmond Safra, Walter Weiner, Jeff Keil, and Dov Schlein—thanks for proving that conservatism and safety pay off in the long run.

The
Mutual Fund
Wealth Builder

1

WINNING THE
NO-WIN GAME

"BONDS IN SLUMP," read the headline in the spring of 1987. One perceived the sound of footsteps heading for the exit door.

"STOCKS PLUNGE 508 POINTS, A DROP OF 22.6%. 604 MILLION VOLUME NEARLY DOUBLES RECORD"—in the front-page headline type normally reserved for wars and the like, the country read the dire news of 20 October 1987. The sounds were more distinct now. It didn't take a rocket scientist to discern the sounds of investors in an advanced state of panic.

"THE DOW PLUNGES 190 POINTS, ABOUT 7% IN A LATE SELLOFF; TAKEOVER STOCKS HIT HARD. IS IT 1987 AGAIN?" This on 14 October 1989, the day after the United Airlines takeover first fell apart. Visualize bathers in a shark-infested swimming pool, and you start to get the idea.

"Stocks fell again yesterday partly in reaction to a 63% dividend reduction by Chemical Banking . . . and since mid-July, when it came within a hairbreadth of reaching 3,000, it has sunk 21.2%." This on 12 October 1990. Yogi

Berra was right: This was déjà vu all over again. Less than three years since the market rushed up to new highs and then swooned.

The rout was on. Many investors would sooner buy a car from Joe Isuzu than listen to the next recommendation from their stockbroker. Didn't we do the patriotic thing—participate in the stock and bond market? They had supported the American economic system—playing mini-capitalists with their $1,000, $10,000, $100,000. The sums did not matter.

They took money intended for vacations, children's education, retirement. Nest eggs, "play money," the rainy-day funds. It didn't make any difference. They were sold on the safety of the investments being recommended to them. "These instruments are backed by the full faith and credit of your state." "Options are an extremely prudent, low-cost method of participating in the stock market." "If you can't believe in IBM, what can you believe in?" "There is nothing safer than U.S. Treasury Bonds."

Hopes, aspirations, plans. All dashed. Uh, uh, this isn't for me. I feel like I'm on a daily roller coaster. The market is up 50 points at noon and closes down 75 points on the day. Have the gods all gone crazy? The game is getting away from the players.

The realization slowly sinks in—they were probably in way over their heads. The stock and bond markets are no longer for the little guy. "In an arena packed with program traders, insurance companies, bank trust departments, investment management boutiques—players who toss around multimillion-dollar trade tickets like Monopoly money—where is there room for me? I was crazy if I thought I had an even chance."

So they head for the exits. What they earn on their newly-opened savings accounts or newly-purchased 3-month Treasury Bills might be less than what they might realize on longer-term bonds or (gasp!) even stocks, but at least now they get to sleep well at night. No longer the fear of being a hero in the morning and a failure by nightfall.

That is all fine and well if one truly believes stock and bond investing has become a no-win situation, a game. Fine, throw in the towel, cash in your chips, stick your head in the sand. Take the money (what's left of it) and run. But, as we shall see later, if you believe all the evidence that shows beyond a shadow of a doubt that over the long term stocks and bonds are the place to be, if you continue to believe in the efficacy of the markets, then some soul searching is in order. First, though, we must try to understand what went wrong, where our thinking was faulty.

MISTAKE NO. 1: FOCUSING ON THE UPSIDE

What turns investors on? "George, I have a stock for you which our analyst believes can double in the next two years." "Ms. Jones, how would you like to earn 9 percent with your principal guaranteed by the U.S. Government?" There are many variations on the theme, but the beat always remains the same. Here is how you might do if things go well. Does any serious businessman ever undertake a venture based strictly on best-case assumptions? But that is exactly what starry-eyed investors are doing by focusing solely or primarily on the upside.

MISTAKE NO. 2: CONFUSING INVESTING WITH FOOTBALL

Vince Lombardi, the legendary coach of the Green Bay Packers, is supposedly the one who coined the phrase, "The best defense is an offense." That may work in football, but it rarely, if ever, does in investing. A pro football game takes place over a finite period of time. It begins at the opening whistle and is over 60 (playing) minutes later. In those circumstances, true, keeping your offense on (and your defense off) the field works. But investing takes place over an open-ended period of time. You don't know at what point you are entering the game (didn't stocks appear to be great buys as the market rushed through 2700 during the summer of 1987 or towards 3000 in the summer of 1990?), nor when you will be leaving.

MISTAKE NO. 3: MISTAKING LUCK FOR TALENT

The 1980s were a heady decade. The stock market was up nine out of ten years, measured by the popular barometers. Average annual returns in equities almost doubled historical norms. Many an advisory-letter writer's and investment manager's reputation was founded on how they did during all or part of this ten-year period. (The same holds true in other areas of investing as well. How many genius and celebrity status reputations were garnered by players in the New York real estate market who simply had the luck of starting at or near the bottom with the depressed values of 1973–74, and riding out the extended up-leg for the ensuing 15 years?).

I do not want to discourse on the pros and cons of the random walk theory—whether markets are truly efficient or not—but be honest with yourself. As moths are attracted to the fire, so the average investor wants to believe that their stockbroker, their investment advisor is brilliant. But a simple test will let a little air out of that balloon. If you can, get a list of the closing prices for all stocks listed on the New York Stock Exchange as of 31 December 1979. Tape it up on the wall. Give a young child—five or ten years old—a dart and ask him or her to throw it at the wall ten times. Check how those ten issues performed over the ensuing decade. Very likely, the child did as well as the gurus. So much for talent!

MISTAKE NO. 4: LOSING SIGHT OF BASIC MATH

Later in this book, we will take a more in-depth look at the simple mathematics of investing. For now, let us focus on but one aspect. I hate to make the equation, but in many respects investing in the stock market is like gambling in a casino. To wit, in the best of circumstances the house always has a slight edge. So this is really not so much a mistake as it is a mathematical trap. I call it the 20/20 trap.

Consider the following: If I told you I had an investment for you which had the potential to appreciate 20 percent in a rising market and to depreciate 20 percent in a slumping market, would that be a break-even situation? The answer is an emphatic *no!* Study Table 1.1.

What poetic justice! Regardless of the sequence (and regardless of the claims to the contrary, no one, repeat no

TABLE 1.1

The 20/20 Trap

SCENARIO 1: Rising Market First	
Starting Value	$ 100
20% Gain	$ 20
	$ 120
Followed by Decline	
20% Loss	$ 24
Ending Value	$ 96

SCENARIO 2: Declining Market First	
Starting Value	$ 100
20% Loss	$ 20
	$ 80
Followed by Rise	
20% Gain	$ 16
Ending Value	$ 96

one, knows whether the investor will first face a bear market or a bull market), the amount of the loss in this seemingly "break even" situation is the same in either case. Sort of like getting paid off 36:1 on a roulette wheel, even though there are 38 possible spots for the ball to land in (0, 00 and numbers 1–36). You are definitely going to lose—it's only a question of time and degree.

MISTAKE NO. 5: "DOUBLING UP" TO RECOUP LOSSES

We don't want to embarrass anyone, so we will not ask for a show of hands. But how many of you fit the following profile, or something akin to it?

With the memory of the mid-1970s still somewhat fresh in your mind, when too-good-to-be-true money market rates in the high teens prevailed, flash forward now to 1983–84. You faced a quandary: money market rates had slumped to the 5–6 percent level. How do you make up for the missing 10 percent in yield? Of your own volition or having been counselled by some securities salesman to do so, you cashed in your CDs, T-Bills or money market funds and put the proceeds into the ABC Government-Plus Bond Fund.

(Aside: while growing up, I had a notion of an authority ladder along the lines of teachers—parents—religious leaders—policemen—government—G——D. It was the mutual fund industry that pointed out to me the error in my thinking, namely that my ladder was missing a rung between government and G——D: government-plus.)

How convenient! Instead of 5–6 percent, you now received a yield of 10–12 percent. Oops, did I forget to tell you, Mr. Customer, you just went from a basically short-term risk-free vehicle to a long-term investment subject to major capital loss should interest rates move against you?

Oh, and "Plus" in the name means we're writing options against the portfolio holdings.

This boosts the yield but mortgages away any potential capital appreciation (if interest rates decline, which would normally result in higher values for the bonds in the portfolio, the purchasers of the options will call away our bonds). Plus (no pun intended), these options offer minimal downside protection; if interest rates rise sharply, the purchasers of the options will simply not exercise their rights. Oh, and one last thing. That 4–6-inch-high number in our ad that you thought was a yield really isn't; it's a "distribution rate." You didn't read the fine print? Well, a distribution rate is current yield plus realized short-term capital gains. (Fortunately for us vendors, interest rates have been declining over the past twelve months, so as we sell positions, we've taken some profits; current yield as *you* know it has only been about 8–9 percent. You can't really expect us to highlight as drab a number as that in our ads.)

Care to guess what happened next? Right: interest rates first declined further, so these funds' nominal yields shrank to single digits. Then, the double whammy—interest rates spiked nearly 2 percent higher in early 1987, causing double-digit percentage losses for investors in such funds. You want your $10,000 back, Mr. Martin, like when you cashed in your CD? Well, there's a little problem. Didn't I explain to you that in a government-bond fund the government only guarantees the principal at maturity, not changes in value due to market fluctuations? You see, your $10,000 is worth only $8,000 now.

But I have just the thing for you. Our firm is bringing out a new closed-end bond fund with a very attractive yield. If you give me the order today, I can guarantee you'll get in at the issue price.

Ever downward we spiral. Here, of course, the investor failed to realize that while the yield at issue price was quite attractive, issue price would last only until those shares began trading—at which point they would be priced less all start-up expenses (including 6–8 percent paid to the salesman). Presto! $10.00 per share becomes $9.20 overnight. More principal gets whittled away.

The final ignominy was yet to come. George, I know we've suffered a couple of setbacks the last few years, but I think I've finally got the answer. If you let me transfer you out of that closed-end bond fund, I can put the proceeds into our high-yield (a.k.a. "junk") bond fund. Not only will it boost your yield by 3–4 percent, but I think we have a good chance to make back all the money we lost on those last two trades. What do you think?

The gullible went along at this last attempt to double up and make it all back. What a horrendous chain. From bank CD/U.S. Treasury Bill to government-plus fund to closed-end bond fund to junk bond fund. How low can you go! That's the definition of a mistake. Is it any wonder that investors look at investing as a no-win game?

So what then is the answer? Is investing really a no-win game? Are investors correct when they cash in their portfolios and stay strictly in short-term instruments?

An emphatic NO!! You can win at investing. Two provisions: you must stay away from the mistakes outlined above, and you must come to accept the notion that the way to win is by not losing.

The true meaning of this latter statement will become apparent over the course of this book. For now, however, let us lay down a few basic principles.

PRINCIPLE NO. 1: LEARN TO SCREW YOUR HEAD ON BACKWARDS

Instead of looking for the stock which will double over the next two years, try to find the investment that will go down in value only half as much as the overall market during a decline. How your portfolio performs in down markets is much more critical to your ultimate success than how it performs during up markets (remember The 20/20 Trap).

This principle is particularly difficult to accept because it goes against every rule of marketing and selling. It is called negative selling. Can you truly expect your broker or advisor to call and say, "I have an investment for you that will only go down half as much as the market if we have a decline"? It means the salesman must admit that markets do go down, which they hate to do. Is the potential for smaller losses something anyone wants to sell? We should live so long!

PRINCIPLE NO. 2: YOU MUST UNDERSTAND THE MEANING OF RISK/REWARD

In the following chapter, we will begin taking an in-depth look at risk—its scope, its elements, its dynamics. To be a successful investor you must come to grips with risk, starting with whether you have the psyche for it. Rewards are beguiling, but they come at a price—risk. You can't get one without coming to grips with the other. It's a package deal—there's no getting away from it.

PRINCIPLE NO. 3: INVESTING SHOULDN'T GENERATE EXCITEMENT

I was once discussing with a reporter the investment approach I will set out for you in this book. After hearing me out she said, "Isn't that awfully boring?" To which I replied, "If making money every year, if going to sleep peacefully every night without a care for my clients' portfolios is boring, then I'm all for boredom." You want excitement? You want the chance to make a quick fortune? Go to Las Vegas or Atlantic City! As I've often said to potential clients who tell me this is "play" money, Wall Street doesn't give you dancing girls, floor shows, or complimentary meals and rooms. Casinos are for excitement; the stock and bond markets are for investing.

PRINCIPLE NO. 4: AFTER EVERY HILL IS A VALLEY

This is very closely related to Principles 1 and 2. Markets don't go straight up. It was uncanny during the early months of 1987 how many forecasts were touted about the market going straight to 3000 or 3500. And again in the early summer of 1990, with the market finally approaching 3000, the talk bandied about was of a 3500 Dow Jones Average by the end of the year. Only in retrospect do we see just how absurd these forecasts were.

No, markets don't go straight up. But the good news is that neither do they go straight down. After every valley is another hill. So if the thought of such a roller coaster ride leaves you with much trepidation, we must find a way to chop off the hills and fill in the valleys.

That is what winning by not losing is all about. Coming to grips with risk/reward. Being aware that our primary goal must be to design portfolios that do well in down markets. Being satisfied with boring, consistent returns and leaving the excitement to others. Ultimately, to enjoy the long-term benefits of stock and bond investing without self-inflicting the pain associated with today's turbulent markets. Done properly, you can have your cake and eat it too. Let's see how it's done.

2

EVERYTHING YOU ALWAYS WANTED TO KNOW ABOUT RISK

THE AVERAGE stockbroker/investment advisor must be a gentleman. How do I know? Gentlemen don't use four-letter words, and brokers/advisors rarely if ever talk about R-I-S-K. Rewards are featured in the bold print, risks in the microscopic type at the bottom (and then only because of demands by regulators). Has a speedreader yet been found who can read the fine-print disclaimer in television commercials for financial products before they disappear from the screen? Doubtful!

No, you're not going to hear much talk about risk from those trying to get you into the investing game. Risk defines the downside, and as we said earlier, no one likes to do negative selling. Yet without comprehending risk, one can never be a truly informed investor. You cannot appreciate the soundness of the principles of winning by not losing without being aware of the effect risk has on the investing process. Let's get started by looking at some basics.

BASIC NO. 1: WHAT DIFFERENTIATES SAVINGS VEHICLES FROM INVESTMENT VEHICLES IS RISK

When you put $10,000 into a savings account, Treasury Bill, or other short-term cash equivalent, you do so with the understanding that at some point you will receive back your initial $10,000 contribution, plus interest for the use of your money by the borrower (the bank or U.S. Government) while they had your money. You also know your $10,000 cannot appreciate and become $20,000 by the time you get your money back (reward), nor can it shrink to $5,000 (risk). Simply put, savings vehicles do not provide the potential for capital gains or losses.

Investment vehicles, on the other hand, do have risk. A $10,000 investment in a stock might eventually be worth a multiple of your initial investment (capital gains), or as many investors painfully learn, a fraction of its starting value (capital loss).

The fact that savings vehicles do not have the potential for capital gains should not be of any concern to you, not if you have a proper understanding of the role savings play in your total financial scheme. What are savings? Savings are your rainy-day funds, your emergency kit. If unexpected expenses come up, if your normal sources of income disappear, where do you turn? To your savings.

To paraphrase the advertising slogan of a well-known overnight delivery firm: savings are the monies that must absolutely, positively be there when you need them. Ergo, they cannot be subjected to risk, because risk equals potential capital loss. Hence, there also is no chance of capital appreciation. But who cares? Your rainy-day account must remain intact; anything you earn by way of interest is "gravy," particularly if it exceeds the inflation rate (more on that later).

On the other hand, the tuned-in investor also realizes that there is little chance of achieving investment goals without incurring such risk. Why? Because the flip side of risk is reward. They are part and parcel of each other. Without the potential for reward—capital appreciation— there is little hope of achieving *long-term* investment objectives. Whether it be to fund a child's higher education or prepare for retirement, risk/reward has the potential to allow us to maintain a certain lifestyle even when extraordinary expenses are incurred (college) or after our regular source of earnings ceases (retirement).

Again, being realistic, we are aware that between the time our investment program begins and the time we begin liquidating our investments for the intended purpose, there will be many ups and downs. This is bearable as long as over time we net out something approximating the historic returns that stocks and bonds have afforded (see Table 2.1). The contrasts, therefore, between savings and investments are stark.

BASIC NO. 2: ALL INVESTMENTS HAVE RISK

Events in recent years have shattered the notion of the "safe haven" investment—government bonds, blue chip stocks, etc. Farewell to investment vehicles that dogma once held you could buy and hold with nary a care in the

TABLE 2.1

Savings vs. Investments

Savings	Investment
Rainy-day fund, sudden emergencies	College, retirement, etc.
Short-term perspective	Long-term perspective
Cannot afford capital loss	Must achieve capital appreciation

world over their safety or ability to provide consistently positive returns. How ironic that on 19 October 1987, the day of the great crash, the then bluest of blue chips—IBM—declined more in value (24 percent) than the overall market (22 percent)!

So Basic No. 2 is getting in touch with reality. Since by definition any and all investments can go down in value, they all have risk. Granted, an investment in U.S. Treasury Bonds, with principal guaranteed by the U.S. Government, might have less risk than an investment in raw land, but that is merely a question of degree, not an absolute. Whatever components you have in your portfolio, each and every one of them contains risk.

As long as we're at it, let's examine some oxymorons that constantly inveigle investors. A "guaranteed investment" or "wealth without risk" are contradictions in terms. Let's take a closer look at each of these. If you accept the premise that all investments have risk, and you also realize that risk equals potential capital loss, how then can you guarantee an investment? Every company that subsequently went bankrupt had in effect guaranteed its debentures when they were first issued. What good did it do you? A guarantee is only as good as the ability of the person or entity providing it to insure that no calamity will befall your investment during the time it is in place, which in itself is an impossibility. (What of the U.S. Government guaranteeing principal in Treasury and Agency bonds? We will deflate that balloon momentarily.)

What of wealth without risk? Wealth ordinarily derives from capital appreciation (reward). Again, the potential for capital appreciation is *always* coupled with the potential for capital loss (risk). You can't have one without the other. If you believe you can achieve wealth without risk, then you probably also believe in tooth fairies.

BASIC NO. 3: RISK IS MULTIFACETED

We often speak of investment risk in a generic sense, in the singular. If we were to be more precise, we should speak of investment *risks,* in the plural. For in fact, as we shall see in the following chapter, there are many different aspects to the risks associated with investing. If we are to win by not losing, each and every aspect must be dealt with individually. An investor dealing with one or a few of these facets will be better off than someone who focuses primarily on the reward side of the equation, but will still be exposed to potential losses emanating from the untended aspects. This makes coping with risk seem particularly problematic. The good news is that each of these problems has a solution, as we shall now see.

3

THE MANY FACES
OF RISK

RISK NO. 1: INFLATION

Inflation is granted first order of priority for a number of reasons. One, it is really a hidden risk and therefore often lulls investors into a false sense of security—its impact is difficult to perceive on a daily, weekly, or monthly basis. If you purchased shares of XYZ Corp. at $100 per share, and you read in the paper that XYZ declined $2 per share yesterday, you know you suffered a 2 percent loss. But if you're an average investor and you read that the GNP deflator for the prior quarter was 2 percent, you don't relate that to the same loss in your portfolio.

Two, the typical investor measures the performance of investments in absolute dollar terms rather than in real terms. You invested $100 one year ago and today it's worth $120. You're up 20 percent. Wrong! You are up 20 percent *less* the amount of purchasing power you have lost as a result of inflation.

When we first equated risk with capital loss, a more precise equation would have been to loss of purchasing power. The insidious side of inflation is that when it seems you're standing still, you're actually falling behind. If your portfolio was worth $100,000 five years ago and it is worth $100,000 today, you did not break even. Why? Inflation. $100,000 today will purchase considerably less goods and services than $100,000 did five years ago. How much less? Check the rate of inflation. In Table 3.1 we see how rapidly such inflation-induced losses accrue.

Planning to retire in fifteen years? If inflation over that time averages no more than 4 percent (which in terms of the current environment would be a significant accomplishment), you can expect the dollars you are putting away today to have lost nearly half of their purchasing power. Sending a child to college in ten years? If inflation begins to ratchet up during that period, say to 8 percent, you may need more than double the amount you currently have available. Finally, a doomsday-type scenario—should inflation rates soar to double-digit levels of 10 percent or more, monies invested in a U.S. Treasury Bond will have depreciated in value (measured in purchasing power) by 85% over 20 years, 91% over 25 years, and 94% over 30 years.

TABLE 3.1

Loss of Purchasing Power Value of $1

Number of Years	Rate of Inflation			
	4%	6%	8%	10%
5	$ 0.82	$ 0.75	$ 0.68	$ 0.62
10	0.68	0.56	0.46	0.39
15	0.56	0.42	0.32	0.24
20	0.46	0.31	0.21	0.15
25	0.38	0.23	0.15	0.09
30	0.31	0.17	0.10	0.06

This is what I meant earlier by a "guaranteed investment" being a contradiction in terms. As is now apparent, the government borrowing $1,000 from you today and guaranteeing to return that same $1,000 in 20 or 30 years is not very much of a guarantee, as long as we live in inflationary times.

Well, you might ask, what of the interest on those bonds? Isn't such income sufficient to offset the loss of purchasing power? The answer is that it might be, but there are a number of "ifs:" *If* you reinvest the interest as received instead of spending it. *If* interest rates at the time you reinvest each interest payment are equal to or exceed the original rate. *If* the rate of inflation over the life of the bond never exceeds that bond's interest rate. Then, and only then, will purchasing power have been maintained. To repeat, not much of a guarantee!

There is, of course, one additional risk associated with such investments, as we said earlier. That is that the guarantee of principal applies only when these bonds are held until maturity. Should you be forced to sell them prior to maturity, you might incur substantial loss of principal if interest rates have risen in the interim—the value of bonds moves in a direction inverse to rates; as rates rise, values fall.

Inflation risk also explains why savings vehicles are poor choices for an investment program. Particularly in the post–October 1987 period, many investors who had been buffeted by the double shock waves of the spring bond debacle and the autumn stock market crash decided such turbulence was no longer for them. They cashed in their equities and fixed-income instruments and placed the proceeds solely into "risk-free" money market vehicles.

How wrong they were! As the chart above drives home, seemingly "risk-free" vehicles have the potential, in fact, to be rather high in risk unless they do a good job of coping with inflation. How good are savings instruments as inflation fighters? The record indicates a rather spotty record.

The data in Figures 3.1, 3.2 and 3.3, compiled by Ibbotson Associates, provide an interesting perspective on a number of issues: 1. the short-term nature of savings, 2. the long-term time frame of investments, 3. the "guarantee" on Government bonds, and 4. the failure of savings instruments as investment vehicles.

1. U.S. Treasury Bills (a fairly accurate barometer of savings rates) do best as inflation fighters over shorter time periods. By the time you get out to 10–20 year moving time frames, they are barely beating inflation half the time. Are you willing to place a 50:50 bet on the ability of your investments to meet your objectives? Hopefully not.

2. Stocks as an inflation-hedge are like fine wine—they improve with age. By the time we get to the longest time periods, they have a perfect score, topping inflation 100 percent of the time, having steadily improved from 1 year out to 20 years.

3. Of the three main investment avenues, "guaranteed" U.S. Treasury Bonds have the most abysmal record as inflation fighters in each average time period studied. Unlike stocks, their performance deteriorates as time frames lengthen. Not surprisingly, there are investment theoreticians who suggest that based on this record, a portfolio should either consist of all equities (for aggressive investors) or equities and cash equivalents; they believe there is no place in the prudent portfolio for bonds. So much for guarantees!

4. Note also that even over the shortest time frame—one year—stocks have a track record similar to Treasury Bills. Even investors approaching their "moment of truth," the time when investments must be liquidated for their intended purpose, need not despair. With as little as one year to go, stocks do no worse than Treasury Bills in protecting the purchasing power of your dollars.

The point is clear. Inflation is perhaps the most signifi-

FIGURE 3.1

The Number of Times U.S. Treasury Bills Equaled or Exceeded Inflation, 1926–1990

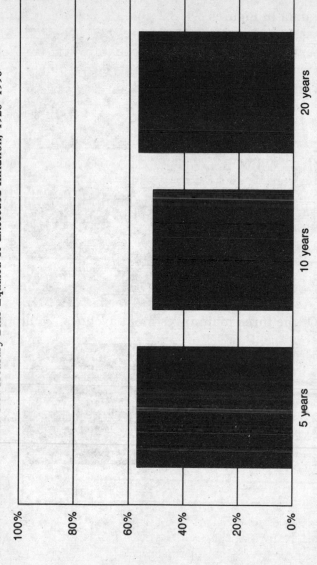

Source: Stocks, Bonds, Bills and Inflation, 1991 Yearbook (Ibbotson Associates Inc., Chicago). Used with permission.

FIGURE 3.2

The Number of Times Common Stocks Equaled or Exceeded Inflation, 1926–1990

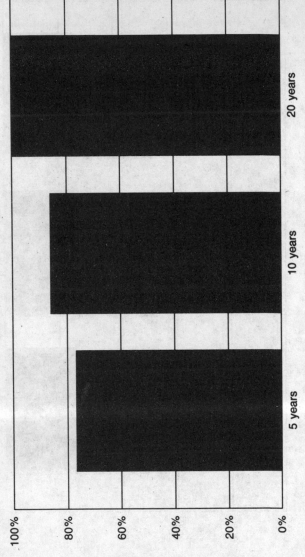

Source: Stocks, Bonds, Bills and Inflation, 1991 Yearbook (Ibbotson Associates Inc., Chicago). Used with permission.

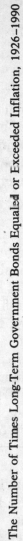

FIGURE 3.3

The Number of Times Long-Term Government Bonds Equaled or Exceeded Inflation, 1926–1990

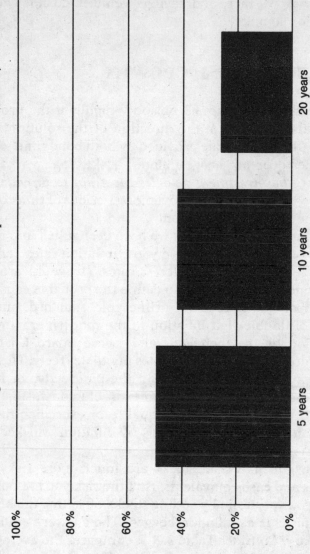

100% 80% 60% 40% 20% 0%

5 years   10 years   20 years

Source: Stocks, Bonds, Bills and Inflation, 1991 Yearbook (Ibbotson Associates Inc., Chicago). Used with permission.

cant risk we face, and savings vehicles do not work as inflation fighters!

SOLUTION NO. 1: GROWTH

Figures 3.1, 3.2, and 3.3 not only highlight the problem; they also point us in the direction of the solution. Obviously, the interest rate provided by both bonds and savings vehicles does not hedge inflation risk. What works best? *Stocks, the investment vehicles most apt to provide sufficient capital appreciation* over long periods of time to combat the scourge of inflation.

Granted, in recent years we have been lulled into a false sense of security by relatively low inflation rates and relatively high short-term interest rates. (It would probably take another entire book to define the probable causes for this aberration—removal of the gold standard, our first taste of double-digit inflation in the modern era, and the decision by the then Federal Reserve Board Chairman Paul Volcker to let interest rates fluctuate freely. These are but some of the suspects.) But the perspective of longer time frames leads us to an inexorable conclusion: Only growth of portfolio values equal to or exceeding the current and forecast future rates of inflation will keep our portfolios whole.

But, you may ask, stocks are much more risky than bonds and cash equivalents. Isn't the risk you are building into your portfolio by adding stocks offsetting the benefits they provide as inflation hedges? The answer is quite the contrary. Consider Table 3.2. It compares the average annual returns and risk levels (using Standard Deviation, or volatility, currently the most widely accepted benchmark of risk) of an all-bond portfolio versus a portfolio comprised of 90 percent bonds and 10 percent stock. As can be seen, even a small exposure to stocks—no more than 10 percent—improves your average annual returns (i.e., im-

TABLE 3.2

Annual Returns

	Bonds	Stocks	90/10 Mix
1981	7.30%	−4.90%	6.00%
1982	31.10	21.60	30.10
1983	8.00	22.50	9.40
1984	15.10	6.20	14.20
1985	21.30	31.70	22.30
1986	15.60	18.60	15.90
1987	2.30	5.20	2.60
1988	7.60	16.50	8.50
1989	14.20	31.60	16.00
1990	8.30	−3.10	7.10
10 Years Annualized	12.80%	13.90%	12.90%
Standard Deviation	8.38	13.19	8.32

proves your chance of beating inflation) and actually reduces risk levels. You can have your cake and eat it too.

RISK NO. 2: LIQUIDITY

Liquidity actually defines two features of an investment: its ability to be converted readily into cash, and the minimal effect on price that liquidation of such an asset should have. We often hear of "liquid" markets, which implies to the potential investors in such markets that these markets are populated with a steady stream of buyers and sellers. No, Mr. Prospect, you'll have no problem converting your assets into cash. Even if we can't find a buyer for you, our specialists or market makers stand ready to pump liquidity into the market when you need it.

To which I for one say "Rubbish." The record of recent years belies this promise. The promise of liquidity has degenerated into the liquidity trap. Remember the old joke, "Sell!" "To whom?" It is no longer funny.

Item: The Singapore Stock Exchange closes for an entire

week in 1986 after the bankruptcy of a major real estate developer.

Item: As mentioned in Chapter 1, the municipal bond market came to a virtual halt in the spring of 1987 as major Wall Street market makers suddenly shut their books and the market was flooded by a rash of sell orders triggered by disillusioned shareholders liquidating their tax-free bond funds.

Item: 19 October 1987. Besides being noteworthy as the day when the stock market collapsed 22 percent, it also marks the day on which many New York Stock Exchange specialist firms ran out of capital and on which over-the-counter market makers stopped answering their phones.

Item: As the catastrophe on Wall Street reverberated around the world, the Hong Kong Exchange stayed closed for the entire week of 19–23 October.

Pardon me, but your shortcomings are showing. A specialist may be empowered to maintain orderly markets, but how can you fault the specialist when he is being trampled to death by a pack of stampeding behemoths (a.k.a. institutional investors)? The same goes for the dealer system, whether market makers in government bonds, municipal issues, or over-the-counter stocks. As far as liquid markets are concerned, perhaps the game has gotten away from the players.

And let us not close the book on this sorry state of affairs without one further glance at an area already beaten to death by many other writers—the junk bond market. It is truly amazing how many years this house of cards was propped up by but one major firm and but one major player! Just long enough for all the culprits and their sycophantic leeches to suck out every possible last cent of ill-begotten profits. How pitiful to look on now as the luckless S & Ls, insurance companies, and other rubes who came under the spell of the swami, wonder what to do with issues for which there is zero liquidity. Sell! To whom?

SOLUTION NO. 2: MUTUAL FUNDS

Let us remember that in dealing with risk, we can never realistically hope to totally remove its effects on our portfolios. Rather, what we are seeking to do is to cope with it as best we can to reduce to the extent possible its impact on our portfolio. This is particularly true when discussing liquidity risk. Obviously, stock and bond markets around the globe are grappling with a growing liquidity crisis. If we as investors must acquire stocks and bonds in order to ensure the achievement of our goals, we must seek out avenues that best shield us from this burgeoning crisis.

Such an avenue is available: *open-ended mutual funds.* When I first began espousing the benefits of investing via mutual funds some sixteen years ago, I often felt like a lone voice in the wilderness. Particularly after the debacles of the "go-go" funds in the late 60s and early 70s, no one looked upon mutual funds as a viable alternative for serious investors. Today, all that has changed. Financial newspapers and magazines carry regular features on the fund industry, while such publications spotlight and interview leading fund managers. Peter Lynch's retirement as the portfolio manager of Fidelity Magellan Fund in the summer of 1990 was as widely covered by the media as any Wall Street–related event in 1990 up to that time.

I suspect, therefore, that I need not provide readers with a primer on mutual funds. Rather, we need focus on only a few key characteristics, particularly those pertaining to the liquidity issue. I specify open-ended funds, because as far as liquidity is concerned, there is a world of difference between open-ended funds and their closed-end cousins. Exchange-listed closed-end funds have all the liquidity risks of exchange-listed (or over-the-counter) stocks.

The open-ended version, by comparison, provides significant hedges against the liquidity trap. The term "open-ended" is self-explanatory. Rather than issuing a finite number of shares or debentures, as would be the case with a normal stock or bond offering, an open-ended fund literally issues and redeems shares on a daily basis. You are dealing directly with the manufacturer—the mutual fund company/distributor itself. If you want to purchase shares, no seller need be found; the company simply issues additional shares. You want to sell? No problem; no buyer must be available. Again, the mutual fund company redeems your shares.

Would not this constant issuing and redeeming of shares in some way dilute the ownership interests of the remaining shareholders? Normally yes, but due to the elasticity of open-ended funds, the answer is no. When you want to purchase shares, the fund's existing pool of capital is expanded and additional shares are issued. When you want to sell, your shares are redeemed, proceeds paid out, and the pool is shrunk. Without a doubt, open-ended mutual funds are the preferred way to satisfy the first definition of liquidity—the ability to readily convert assets into cash.

As to the second feature, i.e. selling having no effect on price, the very fact that open-ended funds are elastic assures this as well. A fund's net asset value, nominally its selling price, is computed daily by taking assets less liabilities and dividing by the number of shares outstanding. Look at Table 3.3.

In this hypothetical example, Mr. Smith owns 1,000 shares of XYZ Fund and decides to redeem his shares. At

TABLE 3.3

Fund Redemptions, XYZ Fund

	Pre-Redemption	Post-Redemption
Assets − Liabilities	$1,000,000	$990,000
Shares Outstanding	100,000	99,000
N.A.V. per Share	$10.00	$10.00

the time his redemption request is received, the Fund has $1 million in net assets (assets less liabilities) and a total of 100,000 shares outstanding. This gives XYZ shares a net asset value (N.A.V.) of $10.00, and makes Mr. Smith's position worth $10,000. By redeeming his shares, the Fund's pool of capital is shrunk by $10,000 to $990,000, its shares outstanding to 99,000 (100,000 − 1,000), leaving its net asset value intact at $10 per share. Liquidity!

As we said earlier, no risk hedge is perfect. Open-ended funds have their flaws as well. On 19 October 1987 many a fund shareholder had difficulty getting through to their funds if they were trying to place redemption orders. But this was not an intrinsic flaw of funds; this was a function of these fund groups having insufficient phone lines and manpower on their order desks. That is a far cry from the investor in a listed stock on that same day attempting to sell and not being able to do so because there were no buyers and the specialist firm in that stock refused to supply any more of their own capital.

I am also often confronted by the challenge: wouldn't a mutual fund overwhelmed by an avalanche of redemption requests, and therefore forced to sell off a substantial portion of its portfolio, face the same bottlenecks as specialists and market makers in stocks and bonds? The answer: theoretically, yes; on a practical basis, no. Let me explain. For a good many years, the stock and bond markets *were* quite orderly and *were* quite liquid by our definition. That has obviously changed in recent years. Why?

This is one man's opinion, but I believe the change is attributable to the reconstitution of the markets from being dominated by a large number of small, individual shareholders to being dominated by a much smaller number of larger, institutional investors (insurance companies, investment management boutiques, bank trust departments, mutual funds, etc.). On many days in recent years, institutional activity—measured by block trades of 10,000 shares or more—accounted for over 90 percent of all trades. This situation is further exacerbated by the fact that managers today are under intense competitive pressure—"What have you done for me lately?" Ergo, out of a fear of missing the proverbial boat, when they see their peers buying, they buy; when they see their competitors selling, they sell. This is also known as "the herd effect." Facing such pell-mell stampedes, orderliness and liquidity are out of the question.

Fortunately for mutual funds, their shareholder lists resemble those of listed stocks twenty or more years ago—a large, diverse number of small shareholders. I know of no open-ended mutual fund whose shares are concentrated in the hands of a few large institutional investors. So theoretically you could have a "run" on a fund, but on a practical basis it's not in the cards for the foreseeable future.

RISK NO. 3: NUMERICAL

This may be termed the classic risk, because it is the one most often associated with the investment process. First, let's set the scene. We live in an age of information overload, a time when people are trying to simplify their lives. I cannot count the number of times I have heard people complain, "I don't understand the statements I get from my broker/advisor. There's too much information. I can't tell how I'm doing. I'm overwhelmed with paper—dividend reports, purchases, sales, splits. It's too much."

How do you simplify your investment life in light of these demands? Why, make your portfolio more compact, of course. Invest in far fewer issues. Sorry, but that is one of the worst mistakes you can make!

Concentrating your portfolio in too few issues is a prelude to disaster. Pick up the business section of your newspaper, and you'll see what I mean. What used to be an isolated incident is now a virtual daily occurrence. I am referring to the sudden, one-day downdrafts in individual issues. American Widget reports lower than expected earnings. Presto! Down 20 percent. Universal Manufacturing is awarded damages by the court far below what investors were expecting. Blink! Down 15 percent. RST Corp. halts merger talks. Shazam! Down 30 percent. Moody's or Standard & Poors unexpectedly lowers the credit rating of National LBO. Watch out! National's bonds decline 10 percent in value.

Earlier, we touched briefly on another aspect of numerical risk—the notion that a compact portfolio is not risky as long as the concentration is in "blue chip" stocks and government bonds. Sorry, but this can prove equally fatal for a number of reasons. One, as previously noted, the market no longer treats blue chips with the same degree of respect once afforded to them. As I pointed out, on a percentage basis IBM did worse than the overall market on 19 October 1987.

Two, what is perceived as blue chip today may not be deemed so tomorrow. Be honest with yourself. If ten or fifteen years ago you were considering putting together a compact, blue chip portfolio of stocks, what issues would you have included? U.S. Steel, Xerox, Dupont, Avon, Bethlehem Steel, etc.? Tables 3.4 and 3.5 show how you would have done in the ensuing years—not exactly blue chip performance.

Compactness may satisfy the need to simplify, but without a doubt it heightens the risk levels in your portfolio. As we will see often in the pages that follow, our human nature is often our own worst enemy as investors. We try to convince ourselves that we are making our portfolios more manageable by investing in fewer issues. Unfortunately, it doesn't work that way. A smaller, concentrated portfolio is more apt to suffer a major loss. By definition, therefore, it is far riskier.

TABLE 3.4

Ten-Year Performances of Selected
Dow Jones Industrials

Corporation	1980–1989 Total Return (%)
Intl Business Machines	9.4
Bethlehem Steel	40.9
General Motors	62.1
Sears Roebuck	72.8
Eastman Kodak	81.0
USX	86.8
American Express	120.3
Aluminum Co. of America	143.2
Minnesota Mining & Mfg.	148.4
General Electric	167.1
Dow Jones Industrial Average	419.0%

TABLE 3.5

Fifteen-Year Performances of Selected
Dow Jones Industrials

Corporation	1975–1989 Total Return (%)
Bethlehem Steel	34.3
American Telephone & Telegraph	110.8
Eastman Kodak	125.1
USX	129.4
Sears Roebuck	149.6
Intl Business Machines	250.3
Procter & Gamble	324.7
Minnesota Mining & Mfg.	342.8
General Motors Corp.	397.6
Du Pont (E.I.) De Nemours	431.5
Aluminum Co. of America	530.8
American Express	561.9
Dow Jones Industrial Average	807.8%

SOLUTION NO. 3: MUTUAL FUNDS

As we shall see again and again, a common thread throughout the different solutions to risk is the concept of diversification. A well-diversified portfolio is less risky. As it pertains to numerical risk in particular, the old adage is definitely true: "There's safety in numbers."

If the risk is to be in too few securities, then the solution is to be in as many as possible. Later we will tackle the question, how much is enough? For the moment, let's keep it simple. If you own but a single stock and it declines in price, your entire portfolio goes down in value. If you spread your assets over twenty issues and one of them goes down in price, only one-twentieth of your portfolio declines in value. Remember, we are attempting to mitigate the pain brought on by risk. Not every stock you purchase will go up in price, therefore, you must own a multitude of stocks, because when the time comes for one of your issues to decline, we don't want it to represent a lion's share of your portfolio.

Why mutual funds? Because mutual funds are *prepackaged diversified vehicles*. Purchasing a single share of a single mutual fund instantly provides you with representative ownership of a broadly diversified group of stocks and/or bonds. If you carry the notion one step further and purchase a portfolio of funds instead of a single fund, then you will have achieved numerical diversification far beyond what is conceivably possible through the direct purchase of stocks and bonds. Few individuals have displayed the skills required to effectively manage a portfolio numbering in the hundreds, if not thousands, of issues. Yet such a degree of diversification is well within the realm of possibility through a portfolio of funds.

So perhaps human nature can be satisfied. A compact portfolio of mutual funds—perhaps no more than 10–20

When Diversification Is Not Diversification

Caution: As we shall see in Chapter 6, great care must be given to the selection of funds for your portfolio. If they are simply selected at random without proper research, you may end up having a portfolio of funds that are all buying and selling the same group of stocks. If there is significant overlap among the portfolio holdings in the funds you randomly purchased, you have *not* done a good job of reducing numerical risk. Plus, you will have incurred much more expense and more sales charges than were warranted. Such a hodgepodge will provide no added value.

---

funds—to satisfy the desire for streamlining, yet maximized numerical diversification at the same time!

RISK NO. 4: ASSET CLASS

Assuming you have now come to grips with the need for numerical diversification, a word of warning. If you do not pay equal attention to asset class risk, you may still encounter significant risk. While there may be safety in numbers, numbers alone don't count. Why?

All investments in a single asset class will generally react similarly to stimuli. If there are any doubts about that principle, consider what I would call the 1987 Asset Class Laboratory. Often we must deal with investment concepts in theoretical terms. Because of what transpired in 1987, we can see the implications of asset class risk on a rather practical level. Let us revisit that fateful year.

First, the spring. As described earlier, we had a "spike" in interest rates—a sharp rise in rates over a very short time span. In this case, nearly 2 percent higher in approximately eight weeks. Let's assume you were a typical income-oriented investor, or one who viewed yourself as ultraconservative. As a result, your entire portfolio was in U.S. Government, high-grade corporate, or tax-free bonds.

You heeded the need for numerical diversification, and so had spread your portfolio across dozens of issues. Were you immune from risk? No! You suffered major losses—in the order of 20–30 percent—because you failed to take cognizance of asset class risk. During a spike in rates, *all* bonds will react negatively in price. Therefore, regardless of whether you owned one bond or fifty bonds, you nonetheless suffered a major loss.

Now, flash forward to the fall of 1987 (no pun intended). In six days, from 12 October to 19 October, the stock market sank 30 percent, 22 percent on the last day alone—Monday the 19th. Let's now assume you were a very aggressive investor and had your entire portfolio in stocks (or even as we saw moments ago, if you were a less aggressive investor, in a portfolio of blue chip stocks). You once again fell into the asset class trap, even if you had applied numerical diversification and had your portfolio spread over dozens upon dozens of issues.

No matter. During the horrific six days you suffered major losses, because when the stock market absorbs so substantial a shock, generally *all* stocks decline in price. Why? To repeat: all investments in a single asset class will generally react similarly to stimuli (positive and negative). We must, therefore, paraphrase the old adage cited earlier: *"In numbers there is safety, but not if they are all in the same asset class."*

SOLUTION NO. 4: MUTUAL FUNDS

To understand how to cope with asset class risk, let's revisit the 1987 Laboratory. Here's a clue: what was the stock market doing while bonds were plunging in the spring? What were bonds doing during the stock market crash in October? Right, they were going in the opposite direction!

In the early months of the year, stocks headed for new highs on a virtual daily basis, even though bonds were sharply lower. Come the fall, we had a mirror image: panic selling in stocks coupled with sharply higher bond prices, the proverbial "flight to safety."

(As a signpost of just how turbulent the markets have become, on the morning of 20 October, "the morning after," some longer-term U.S. Government bonds opened as much as 8½ points higher. In dollar terms, that is $85 on a $1000 par bond. By comparison, prior to October, 1979 and the appointment of Paul Volcker as Federal Reserve Board Chairman, a changeover that allowed interest rates to fluctuate widely, *daily* price quotes for bonds were sixty-fourths of a point, or 15 cents per bond. In eight years we had gone from daily price changes of 15 cents to opening price moves of $85. That's turbulence!)

Lesson: Regardless of your investment objectives, you should always have a variety of asset classes in your portfolio.

The most conservative, income-oriented investors should own some stocks; the most aggressive, growth-oriented investors should have some bonds. Lest you conservatives fear that a stock-bond portfolio is "riskier" than an all-bond portfolio, remember what we pointed out (p. 25) about the higher average returns and *lower* risk of a 10% stock/90% bond mix versus 100% bonds.

True, there have been times in recent years when stocks and bonds have moved in the same direction. But asset class diversification is not limited solely to stocks and bonds; you can even use cash equivalents (and, although it is beyond the scope of this book, other asset classes such as real estate); and over the long history of investing, stocks and bonds have generally moved in opposite directions, such as in the spring and fall of 1987.

To see the basic soundness of asset class diversification, consider this. Let us say you decided to take a year-long sabbatical in 1987 and did not want to worry at all about your portfolio. If on 31 December 1986 you called your broker/advisor with instructions to put one-half of your assets in stocks and one-half in bonds, or alternatively one-third in stocks, one-third in bonds, and one-third in money market instruments. You added one further proviso: regardless of what transpired during the year, no one was to tamper with the requested asset class mix (later on we shall discuss the relative pros and cons of this approach to asset allocation, also referred to as "fixed mix").

Guess what happened when you checked the financial pages of your newspaper upon your return on 1 January 1988? You would have discovered that your portfolio had actually risen in value during your absence! How much you gained would have been a function of which specific investments you had purchased in your portfolio. In terms of the stock and bond market, you missed the greatest roller coaster ride in modern times. You missed a stock market that one day was headed for new highs and the next for new lows. You missed a bond market suffering the largest losses in its history. Yet you came out ahead (remember how we cautioned earlier about confusing excitement with prudent, risk-averse investing)—all because you protected yourself with asset class diversification.

There is, however, one fly in the ointment. While we look at stocks and bonds in general terms as asset classes, the reality is much more complex. There is no longer a stock market; there is a series of submarkets composed of different classes of stocks (high-cap, low-cap, growth stocks, basic value stocks, etc.). Often they do not move in tandem. Even though all stocks were suffering losses during 1990, the amount of loss depended on the class of stock in which you were invested. If you were invested in the high-capitalization issues that dominate the Standard and Poor's (S&P) 500 for the full year, you suffered losses of approximately

3.1 percent. On the other hand, if over that same time period your stock portfolio was concentrated in the smaller-cap issues that predominate in the National Association of Securities Dealers Automated Quote (NASDAQ) index of over-the-counter issues, your losses approximated 20 percent, six times the high-cap submarket.

The same holds true for bonds. It is now a fragmented series of subsets: Government bonds (long-term, intermediate-term, short-term, mortgage-backed, agency), corporate bonds (investment-grade, junk, same three maturity ranges as Governments, callable, noncallable, fixed, convertible, etc.). Often these subsets head in the same direction but not to the same degree. In the infamous first half of 1987, long-term Government bonds sank 20–25 percent during the spike; curiously, lower-grade corporates (a.k.a. "junk") suffered but minimal losses.

The point is, asset class diversification properly employed should take cognizance of these subsets—which is why I once again recommend mutual funds as the most efficient means of applying true asset class diversification. Imagine the dimensions of a portfolio composed of a minimum 10–12 high-cap stocks, 10–12 low-cap stocks, 10–12 basic value issues, 10–12 growth issues, a dozen Government bonds of various maturities, one or two dozen corporate bonds of various maturities and grades, and so on. Mind boggling to say the least!

Instead, a carefully constructed portfolio of funds can capture as many or more subsets of stocks and bonds in a much more compact, effective manner. Fortunately for investors, the mutual fund industry has evolved into a large number of specialty funds. True, there yet remain some general-purpose funds attempting to be all things to all people. For the most part, however, mutual funds today focus on a given area of expertise (generally one of the subsets mentioned above).

If you want to incorporate convertible bonds into your

asset class diversification matrix, you can either purchase a few dozen individual issues or, preferably, shares in a single one of the more than a dozen convertible bond funds currently available. You believe your diversification should include high-tech stocks? Buy a dozen or so individual stocks, or buy shares in a single high-tech mutual fund. Which sounds more efficient to you?

Conclusion: Regardless of one's objectives, numerical diversification alone will not suffice. Asset class diversification, taking into account as many subsets of stocks and bonds as possible, is incumbent and prudent. The most efficient means of incorporating both numerical and subset asset class diversification into one's portfolio is via a carefully constructed portfolio of mutual funds.

RISK NO. 5: MANAGER

Of all the forms of investment risk we are surveying, this one is perhaps the most sublime. Why? Because here you take a supposedly wise step, only to find it blows up in your face. Let me explain.

You see how complex, time consuming, and intricate prudent investing has become. You realize your own limitations in terms of training, time, discipline. Solution: give your broker discretionary power over your account or hire a full-time professional investment manager. Problem solved.

Wrong! With such a step you have probably built into your portfolio a ticking time bomb, and it is merely a question of time until it will explode. Why? Let me share some trade secrets with you.

I am a full-time portfolio manager. Yet I am not in possession of a crystal ball, nor of the 1 January edition of next year's *Wall Street Journal.* I cannot tell you with 100 percent assurance whether the economy is entering a growth phase or a recession, whether interest rates are headed higher or lower, whether equity prices are going to rise or fall, etc.

How do portfolio managers function? They assemble teams of professionals with many years of combined (and, we hope, complementary) expertise. Periodically (twice weekly, weekly, monthly), they, their associates and staff will sit down and reach conclusions. The economy is expanding, therefore stocks will rise in value. The Federal Reserve Board is about to ease, therefore interest rates will come down and bond prices will rise. The recession is almost over, so cyclical stocks are a good buy.

What are such conclusions? They are forecasts and projections. "Forecasts" and "projections" in the absence of a crystal ball are high-falutin ways of saying "guesses." Admit it, your broker guesses, your portfolio manager guesses. The depth of expertise within their organizations will determine how educated their guesses are. But guesses all the same. What is the likelihood you will be able to find a broker or portfolio manager who guesses right all the time or even most of the time?

Let me save you the trouble. *You are more likely to discover the Loch Ness monster or the Yeti than the proverbial all-weather manager.* In the Greek classics, a common theme was the Siren songs that enraptured and captivated hero after hero. In modern times, the song of the Sirens is the myth of the all-weather manager—the supposed individuals or firms who will steer your portfolio through thick and thin, through bull markets and bear markets, through economic expansions and contractions.

Pshaw! They simply don't exist, or if they do, they are so few in number that the likelihood of finding them is equal to finding the one stock or the one bond that will serve you well in all market environments. Need some proof?

In 1982, the Becker Funds Evaluation Survey (at that time probably the largest pension consulting outfit in the

United States) ran a test of hundreds of the nation's most prominent pension management firms. These are the prestigious, highly regarded firms managing the pension plans of the Fortune 500, state and municipal plans, and other large pools of capital. The test: how many of these industry lions had ranked in the top 25 percent, the top quartile of their peer group for eight consecutive years 1974–1981 (a fair definition of an all-weather manager?). The answer: 0.2 percent!! For those who still confuse excitement with investing, that means you have a *500:1* chance (100%:0.2%) of finding the all-weather manager for your portfolio. Regardless of the game, a casino will give you better odds than that!

Before you retort that the 1982 study was a statistical fluke, let me provide you with some further documentation regarding this myth. The successor to the Becker Funds Evaluation Survey, the SEI Funds Evaluation Survey, has for some time now provided its clients with an offshoot of the 1982 study called "The Consistency Report." Its contents have proven to be as revealing as the earlier work. For instance, the 1989 report documented that among the country's leading portfolio management firms only 12 percent had managed to rank in the top quartile but half the time in the previous ten years.

More revealing yet, and to this observer most embarrassing, *51 percent of these firms had managed to rank in the top half half the time.* Meaning, if you hand over the reins of your portfolio to a single money manager or broker and want to know how he or she will likely perform in the year ahead, you might as well flip a coin! Heads, there will be an above-average year; tails, below-average. Cynical, but true.

That is manager risk. One source of guesswork having complete control over your portfolio. On a regular basis the financial press is filled with stories of once-great managers who suddenly hit a slump. They raise cash as the market is about to head sharply higher. They load up on cyclicals just prior to a recession. They sell oil stocks just prior to an energy crisis.

With the speed with which events are unfolding today; with time frames for market cycles having imploded (do you remember the one about market cycles taking three to five years?); with the roller coaster–type stock and bond markets we currently face; is it any wonder that more and more of the once-great have stumbled and fallen? Manager risk, plain and simple.

SOLUTION NO. 5: MUTUAL FUNDS

This is becoming repetitive, but valid all the same. The solution to manager risk is diversification: never allowing a single manager, broker, management firm to call all the shots; never relying on a single source of guesswork to determine the success or failure of your investment program.

Again, the most efficient way to incorporate manager diversification into one's portfolio is via mutual funds. Each fund has its own manager or management firm. By extension, then, a carefully constructed portfolio of funds will give you exposure to a broad cross-section of investment styles and techniques.

One of the most attractive features of mutual fund investing is that small investors can access the same management expertise for their portfolios as their much larger counterparts in the nation's leading pension offices. The pension officer of a Fortune 500 company can hand over $100 million for a privately managed portfolio to Delaware Investment Advisers; you purchase $1000 of Decatur Fund, Delcap Fund, or Delchester Bond Fund and attain the same management. The trustees of a major endowment employ Neuberger & Berman to manage $50 million of

> ### Caution
>
> As I warned in regard to numerical diversification, great care must be given to prevent overlap in achieving manager diversification via mutual funds. Particularly when purchasing a number of funds from the same fund family, one may discover all funds have the same basic composition—each portfolio manager is selecting purchases from the same "approved list." I will expand on this issue in much greater detail in Chapter 6.

their assets; you invest $2500 in Guardian Fund, Manhattan Fund, or Partners Fund and your assets will be managed the same way. The pension officer of a multibillion dollar state plan selects Capital Guardian Trust to manage a $250 million portfolio; buy shares in Investment Company of America, Amcap Fund, or any other growth fund offered by the American Funds group, and you are on an equal footing.

Mutual Funds Managed by America's Leading Money Managers

A Sampling

Alliance Capital Management L.P.
Associated Capital Investors
Bankers Trust Company
Baring International Investment Ltd.
Barrow, Hanley, Mewhinney and Strauss
Batterymarch Financial Management
Sanford C. Bernstein & Co., Inc.
The Boston Company, Inc.
Capital Guardian Trust Company
Chase Investors Management Corp.
Citibank, N.A.
Cypress Capital Management

Delaware Investment Advisers
Dillon Read Capital Inc.
Fidelity Management Trust Co.
Franklin Portfolio Associates
Goldman Sachs Asset Management
G. T. Capital Management, Inc.
INVESCO Capital Management
John Hancock Financial Services
Hill Samuel Investment Advisers Ltd.
Kleinwort Benson International Investment Ltd.
Lazard Frères Asset Management
Lincoln Capital Management Co.
Loomis, Sayles & Co.
Lord, Abbett & Co.
MacKay-Shields Financial Corp.
Mellon Bank N.A.
Merrill Lynch Asset Management
Mitchell Hutchins Asset Management Inc.
Morgan Grenfell Investment Management Inc.
J.P. Morgan Investment Management Inc.
Nomura Capital Management, Inc.
Pacific Investment Management Co.
Rowe Price-Fleming International, Inc.
Schroder Capital Management International Inc.
State Street Research & Management Co.
Warburg, Pincus Counselors Inc.
Weiss, Peck & Greer
Wellington Management Co.
Western Asset Management Co.

(Also beyond the scope of this book, but I believe even those with billions of dollars to invest are better served by a multifund portfolio than a multi-manager portfolio. Ease of administration, compactness, transition costs from manager to manager, opportunity costs, and so on.)

RISK NO. 6: INTERNATIONAL

Sorry, but the bad news gets worse. Here again, a seemingly wise step—adding international investments into your portfolio in order to diversify—turns against you. If we were to be more precise, the risk is not in international investing, but in the second half of the package—foreign exchange (f/x as it is known in professional circles). This is a package deal that cannot be purchased piecemeal. And while the one, international diversification, makes considerable sense, the other, foreign exchange, is a trap waiting to spring.

How unfortunate for ill-informed investors that in the late 80s, the very same period of time when they were being duped into believing that government-plus bond funds were the equal of T-Bills and CDs, they were falling prey to the surreal returns of international stock funds. If the type size used in print advertising to feature yields on bond funds was extraordinarily large, it paled in comparison to that used for annual returns on international funds.

To appreciate the nature of the trap, a layman's primer on foreign exchange is in order. There is now an extremely active and volatile foreign exchange market. It is the market through which you, your broker or advisor must convert your currency—U.S. dollars—into that used in the country in which you wish to invest before you can buy stocks traded in that country. For instance, if you wish to invest $10,000 in French stocks and the exchange rate for French francs at that time was 5 francs to the U.S. dollar, you could purchase 50,000 francs worth of French stocks. If the particular stock you had in mind was trading at 50 francs per share, you could purchase 1,000 shares.

Now, the trap. A month later you decide to sell; perhaps you feel international investing is not for you. You check with your broker and discover that the per share price had not changed; ABC Français is still at 50 francs per share. Whew! You let out a big sigh of relief. Nothing lost, except some time and commissions. Wrong! Before you get too relaxed, you better check the exchange rate.

If during the month, the exchange rate had shifted to 6 francs per U.S. dollar, then although your sales proceeds will be the same 50,000 francs (less commissions) that you invested a month earlier, when you now convert those francs back into dollars, you will only receive $8,333. The price of your shares didn't change, but you suffered a 17 percent loss!

Are you starting to get the picture? The operation may very well be a success, but the patient may still die. Even if your shares appreciate in value in local currency terms, but the dollar is appreciating at a faster rate versus that currency, *you are going to suffer a loss!*

What occurred in the mid-80s was extremely fortunate from the salesman's point of view. Stock markets around the globe were rising sharply, and simultaneously the U.S. dollar was in a virtual free-fall. (There, again, the substance of a totally separate book. Recall, if you will, the decision of the G-7—the U.S. and its six major trading partners—to intentionally weaken the dollar. It was "too strong," whatever that might mean. Lo these many years later, and we are yet waiting for the supposed benefits of this insane debasement to surface!)

The outcome in the mid-80s, though, was the best of all possible worlds, a true best-case scenario. Rising equity values coupled with rising values for the local currencies. It did not take vendors of these products long to catch on to this golden opportunity. Presto! Skyscraper-size type highlighting 30–40–50–60 percent annual returns. No mention *anywhere* in those ads that over 50 percent of the reported gains was the result of a plummeting dollar, and that ex the foreign exchange factor, these funds were doing no better than their U.S. counterparts, since the domestic stock market was rising quite nicely as well. Caveat emptor!

How risky is the foreign exchange game? Let me share a few vignettes with you. In one of my first economics courses in college (if memory serves me well, it was a class taught by Professor Chang, who confused the dickens out of us with constant references to "General

Moto"), the teacher opined there were only five people in the entire world who understood the concept of money. The problem is we don't know who those five people are! Maybe those five unknown persons are capable of investing in currencies.

The second vignette I call my "wet salt" story: In nineteenth-century Russia, a man entered a store to purchase a sack of salt. The merchant sold it to him at an extremely attractive rate.

The next day he returned to the store in a most agitated state. "You're a thief!" he accused the store owner.

"What do you mean?" the merchant replied. "I sold you that salt very cheaply."

"But it was soaking wet," the customer retorted.

"So?"

"So? How am I supposed to use wet salt?"

"Oh," the store owner now understood. "That salt was not for using; it was for trading!!"

The same may be said for the foreign exchange markets: they are for trading, not for investing. In 1981 I joined a major international bank. The head of our foreign exchange desk described it to me in such terms when I inquired how I as an investment manager could prudently invest in foreign exchange on behalf of my clients. His message: you don't invest in foreign exchange!

Talk to most foreign exchange traders, and they will tell you that most, if not all, of their positions are hedged or closed out by the end of business each day. The risks are simply too high to carry open positions for longer than twenty-four hours. This is one arena in which the game may truly have gotten away from the players. Once dominated by central banks and worldwide commercial banks, today speculators, traders, and futures exchanges control the marketplace.

So, while savvy participants have time frames measured

in hours and at most days, the unsuspecting investor attempting international diversification becomes a long-term participant in what should at best be a short-term foray. Is it any wonder that many of the larger pension-plan sponsors who were the earliest U.S. entrants into international diversification, are now employing separate advisors to hedge out the currency risk in their portfolios? If their international stock manager has $50 million of their capital invested in Japan, their currency manager will hedge an equal amount in yen. If Japanese stocks are truly a good investment, it should not be based on how the yen performs relative to the U.S. dollar.

If currency/foreign exchange risk were the sole component in international risk, the picture would be bleak enough. Unfortunately, it does not end there. For in reality, this is a three-headed monster. Each in its own right presents a problem; combined, they are a virtual risk juggernaut.

1. *Currency.* Enough said.

2. *Stock selection.* Managers of U.S. stock funds have quite a task. They must assess the merits of issues listed on the New York Stock Exchange, American Stock Exchange, regional exchanges, NASDAQ, et al. Literally thousands. Go international and you've compounded the problem manyfold. Tokyo, London, Frankfurt, Milan, Singapore, Hong Kong, etc., etc., etc. We are now in the tens of thousands of potential issues. Can any one firm or individual cover so vast a waterfront?

3. *Liquidity.* We have already described the 1986 debacle in Singapore and its 1987 counterpart in Hong Kong: One week closures while they got their acts together. If in either case you grew queasy and wanted out, impossible. You were literally locked in; the door had been bolted.

Nor is this phenomena particular to the "fringe" markets. Some years ago I met with the president of a major London-based money management firm that in conjunc-

Why Invest Internationally in the First Place?

Follow me: you earn dollars, save dollars, and will likely retire in dollars (or spend dollars for whatever purpose your investment program is intended). If you don't invest internationally, at worst it's an opportunity cost (if over the span of your investment program, foreign currencies had done better than the dollar or foreign stock/bond markets had done better than the U.S. markets, then at the conclusion of your program you could have had more dollars available). On the other hand, if you invest internationally and the dollar outperforms foreign currencies or foreign markets underperform the U.S., you may have substantially impaired your ability to meet your objective.

I agree that for investors from countries with unstable economic systems and fragile political structures, facing double or triple-digit inflation and constant devaluations, not knowing where or in which currency they will eventually spend their wealth, there is no choice (nor is there anything more prudent) but to diversify their portfolios on an international scale. But, fortunately, that is not our case!

We live in a stable economic and political system. Only rarely have we faced even low double-digit inflation, and the vast majority of us will retire on these shores. Why then invest overseas? One last thought: if there are so many golden opportunities overseas, why are savvy investors from around the world shipping their money en masse over here for investing? In case you haven't noticed, they're buying up virtually everything that doesn't move! Farmland, office buildings, golf courses, U.S. Treasury Bonds, auto plants, department stores, food companies. But we're being told the opportunities are elsewhere. Something doesn't jibe.

tion with one of our largest fund complexes was managing one of the top five (by asset size) international stock funds in the U.S. He prided himself on the fact that they had appreciably reduced risk by not allowing any single position in the portfolio to exceed 3 percent of the fund's total assets.

My question to him was simple: if there were a rash of liquidations by his fund's shareholders, and they suddenly had to raise a large sum of money, how long would it take to sell the ten largest positions in his portfolio and not affect the price of those issues (remember our two definitions of liquidity)? This also assumes that other such funds are not simultaneously facing similar selling pressures. His answer, offered rather sheepishly: two to three months.

"Readily convertible to cash?" Hardly. The argument often proffered in favor of international investing is that over 50 percent of world stock market capitalization now resides outside the United States. Fine, except the less than 50 percent inside the U.S. is primarily concentrated in the New York Stock Exchange, while the 50+ percent non-U.S. is dispersed over a wide array of markets scattered around the globe. Our market is hardly perfect (see Risk No. 2), but it shines in comparison to its overseas peers.

SOLUTION NO. 6: PREFERENCE A: HEDGE OUT CURRENCY RISK

As mentioned above, larger investors cognizant of the foreign exchange element in international investing have taken to hedging out all currency exposure in their overseas stock and bond portfolio. This makes it a pure diversification play; however, the elements of selection risk and liquidity risk detailed earlier remain.

PREFERENCE B: GLOBAL MUTUAL FUNDS

This alternative, although it too does not mute selection and liquidity risks, also answers the currency question—particularly for smaller investors with insufficient assets to employ the services of a foreign exchange hedging firm. First, an explanation of terms. An *international* fund is generally one that can invest in all markets *except* the U.S., nor is it generally allowed to hedge currency exposures. By comparison, a *global* fund can invest in all markets *including* the U.S. (to what degree will generally be spelled out in the fund's prospectus) and/or hedge out foreign exchange exposure.

So, if you feel you want to invest internationally, the way to do it is via global funds. You will enjoy all the risk-diluting tendencies of funds enumerated previously. Plus, you hope the portfolio manager has the good sense when he sees the U.S. dollar is exceptionally strong to invest a higher proportion of the overall portfolio in U.S. issues or to hedge a substantial portion of his non-U.S. holdings against the dollar.

This is not even close to being a perfect solution, but it is the best available. In addition to which you might say: "All along, you've been counselling us to watch out for overlap. If I own both domestic stock funds and global stock funds, is there not a good chance that they will both own the same U.S. issues?" A valid question, but my answer would be as follows: (1) If the global portfolio manager is wise enough to be in U.S. issues when the dollar is gaining strength, then the marginal costs of overlap would be more than offset by the substantial foreign exchange losses that were sagely dodged. (2) The manager might employ currency hedges, rather than purchase U.S. stocks, as a reaction to a stronger dollar. In that case, there is no overlap at all.

RISK NO. 7: LOSSES

This caption confuses you. You thought risk is what brings about losses. Now I'm telling you that losses are a form of risk. How can that be? Which is it? Let me explain.

True, other forms of risk—numerical, asset class, manager, etc.—can result in losses. But losses themselves are a risk—the risk being that they so disrupt the investment program that it becomes a virtual impossibility to get back on a proper or desired growth track. In particular, we are talking about *large* losses. Experiencing losses is part and parcel of investing; remember risk/reward. Only starry-eyed believers in investment gurus think they can come through a series of bear markets unscathed.

Realists, or those who have been involved in investments for many years, are well aware of the downside. The investment markets are a series of hills and valleys. The danger we are focusing on now involves those who fall too deep into the valley. Coming to grips with the risk of (large) losses can be achieved through a series of steps.

1. The 20/20 Trap. Remember when we first presented this mischievous trap (p. 5)? It was clear that a seemingly even bet is always a losing bet. Look at it another way (see Table 3.6). Clearly, even bets of whatever dimensions *always* are a losing proposition. Look, however, *very* carefully at the right-hand column of Table 3.6. Notice the rate of acceleration in the amount you are actually behind as the size of the bet grows. In today's market, even if you have not taken proper cognizance of all the risks earlier in this chapter, is there any doubt in your mind that losses of 30–40–50 percent are possible, no, probable? Of course they are! And where does that leave you? How much

TABLE 3.6

Gain (%)	Loss (%)	Net Loss (%)
10	10	1
20	20	4
30	30	9
40	40	16
50	50	25

growth will then be required simply to get back to your starting point?

2. Getting Out of a Hole. This is such a critical concept, it is worth going through methodically. If you start with $100 and suffer a 50 percent loss, you need a 100 percent gain—double—to break even. If you suffer a 20 percent loss, the gain required to offset it is 25 percent greater (see Table 3.7). *Larger losses are much more difficult to offset than smaller losses.* It is not a straight-line progression. A 50 percent loss is nine times more difficult to overcome (not five times) than a 10 percent loss.

Looked at from a different angle, losses erode your capital base. The smaller the capital base, the lower the potential for desired capital growth. To make $50 on a $100 capital base requires a 50 percent gain. Achieving $50 of growth on a $50 base requires a 100 percent gain.

3. Getting Out of a Hole, Then Hitting a Target. Case 1:

TABLE 3.7

Loss (%)	Gain to Offset (%)	Gain/Loss Ratio
50	100	2.00
40	67	1.67
30	43	1.43
20	25	1.25
10	11	1.10

You start with $100,000 and determine that in five years you will need $161,000 for your objective. This equates to a 10 percent annual rate of return. Quite reasonable. But what if you suffer a loss in the first year? What order of growth is required in the remaining four years to hit your target? (See Table 3.8.)

Not a very pretty picture. Suffer a 30 percent loss (remember October 1987 or the summer of 1990) and it will take over 23 percent average annual growth in the remaining four years simply to average 10 percent over the full five years. What if you were slightly more ambitious?

Case 2: You want your money to double in five years' time. You will need slightly less than a 15 percent annual return for such a goal. Same situation—a loss comes first (see Table 3.9).

Is it starting to sink in now? Do you see the risk of losses, especially large ones? A 30% loss needs 30% gains for four consecutive years to hit a 15% annual target! You almost feel as if the deck is stacked against you. And it will be, unless you understand the concept of risk, curbing it, and winning by not losing.

And before you comfort yourself by saying that that only pertains to growth-oriented investors with high targets, let's look at an income investor who suffers a capital loss.

TABLE 3.8

10% Average Annual Growth

First Year Loss (%)	Annual Gain— Last 4 Years (%)
10	15.7
20	19.1
30	23.2
40	28.0
50	34.0

TABLE 3.9

15% Average Annual Growth

First Year Loss (%)	Annual Gain— Last 4 Years (%)
10	22.1
20	25.7
30	30.0
40	35.1
50	41.4

Case 3: A retired person receiving various annual payments from pensions, Social Security, and life insurance needs $8,000 more from her investments in order to make ends meet. With $100,000 to invest, this equals an 8 percent return, which seems quite reasonable. What happens if there is a capital loss (remember those government-plus, closed-end bond funds, et al.)? See Table 3.10.

This is the downward spiral we described in Chapter 1. As you suffer losses, you must get into ever more risky investments if you are to maintain your income level. If your capital erodes by 50 percent, you must either get by on $4000 less if you stay in instruments that yield 8 per-

TABLE 3.10

Starting Value: $100,000
Desired Income: $8,000
Average Return: 8%

Loss (%)	Remaining Capital (RC)	$8000/RC (%)
10	$90,000	9
20	$80,000	10
30	$70,000	11
40	$60,000	13
50	$50,000	16

cent or reinvest in higher yielding, riskier investments. Damned if you do, damned if you don't! As we said, it's not a pretty picture at all.

Let's summarize: *If you're investing, you are sure to experience losses at some point in time. The larger the losses you experience, the much more difficult it will be to overcome them.*

SOLUTION NO. 7: LIMIT LOSSES

Remember once again, we are trying to be realists. Losses are part and parcel of the investing game (unless you believe in tooth fairies or achieving wealth without risk). Losses derive from risk, and risk is multifaceted. However, each of these facets has had a solution, and the solution in each case allowed us to diffuse the risk and thereby lower the potential loss.

Now, we are going a step further in our thinking. We not only want to lower the potential of sustaining a loss; we want to significantly lower the possibility of a *major* loss. Why? Because if we build a portfolio that in the worst of times sustains only minor losses, we can live with it.

Go back to Table 3.6. A 10:10 bet only leaves you with a 1 percent loss. Move forward to Table 3.7. A 10 percent loss only requires an 11 percent gain to break even. On to Table 3.8: a 15.7 percent annual return for four years will result in an annualized return of 10 percent over five years, *if* the first-year loss was no more than 10 percent. Do you see the pattern? Don't go too deep into the valley, and you will not have that difficult a task coming out.

If all facets of risk have been properly diversified away with the solutions previously provided, by definition you will likely have limited your losses. In many cases, I have suggested the use of mutual funds as the most efficient means of incorporating such diversification into your portfolio. In fact, there is a particular category of funds we will soon focus on as the preferred route. For now, let us simply designate them as the "tortoise" funds.

The remainder of this book will be devoted to showing you how to build a portfolio that should keep your losses in check during bear markets and achieve reasonable gains in bull markets. With all due respect to Coach Lombardi, investing is *not* football. If your portfolio limits risk, it will do well in down markets (by limiting losses). If you do well in down markets, you don't have to be a hero in the up markets.

We've covered quite a bit in this chapter, so let's summarize:

- All investments have risk.
- The antidote to risk is diversification.
- The greater the risk, the greater the amount of diversification required.
- Different facets of risk require different types of diversification.

Facet	*Diversification*
Inflation	Growth investments
Liquidity	Mutual funds
Numerical	Mutual funds
Asset class	Funds from different asset classes
Manager	Funds with different managers
International	Global funds (?)
Losses	"Tortoise" funds

- Hirsch's three rules of investing: Diversify, Diversify, Diversify.
- You can never have enough diversification.

Let's close with that thought. Academicians ponder about an "efficient threshold" of diversification. But in their minds, they are debating whether there comes a time when too much diversification will dilute potential returns. That's fine, if you're attempting to maximize upside potential. We're not; we're trying to limit downside losses, and it's clear that the more diversification you have in your portfolio, the lower the probabilities of suffering a major loss. So, if you must err, err to the side of excess.

4

THE TORTOISE HUNT

WHAT DO I mean by tortoise funds? The reference, of course, is to the famous Aesop fable regarding the tortoise and the hare. As we shall see shortly, in the mutual fund universe there is a clear line of demarcation that separates the tortoises (slow, steady plodders delivering median-plus performance) from the hares (spectacular performance for one or two years, then the crash).

Common sense: if you would like your portfolio to deliver a safe, consistent performance, the components that make up the portfolio should be safe and consistent. This is particularly true if time and inclination leave you with no other alternative but to have a limited (less than ten?) number of funds in your portfolio. In a limited-size portfolio, one fund out of five varying widely from course can cause the entire portfolio to miss its target.

(Those who profess that investing is a science rather than an art would offer an alternative to the tortoise portfolio. Their idea relates to what is known as "correlation

coefficients." In layman's terms: If you can trace performance characteristics of various investment instruments in
different environments, then by blending them together in
different proportions you can get the same desired consistent results. As a simplistic example, if Fund A generally
rises 25 percent while Fund B is declining 10 percent, and
vice versa, then if you own both Funds A and B you will
generally always net out a 15 percent gain.)

Does slow but steady win the race? Absolutely! It did in
the fable and it does in the real world of investing today.
The greater the turbulence, the greater the premium that
should be placed on consistency. The home-run hitter may
garner the headlines, but more often than not, it is the
singles and doubles hitters who win ball games.

Therein, however, lies one of the problems of the tortoise hunt, one that we will examine further in the next
chapter. Namely, tortoises don't make headlines. If you are
going to rely on the popular press to feature funds that you
may wish to include in your portfolio, forget it! They like
to feature the hares, the home-run hitters. Do you think
tortoises ever get featured among the funds with the best
performance for the last three months? Hardly.

The headlines go to the stars of the moment, the funds
that were up 25 percent for the quarter while the overall
market rose but 10 percent. Are these stars, or novas, a
great flash of light, followed by burnout? Andy Warhol had
a great saying about everyone being famous for fifteen
minutes. In the mutual fund world, fame generally lasts
not much longer than three months.

You know those news magazines that have "Where Are
They Now" columns about personalities from the past? The
financial press would be performing a true public service
if it ran a similar column on former hares that were featured three, six, or twelve months prior. Where are they
now? Would you care to guess? The hares eventually all
stop running.

It requires considerable gullibility to believe that any fund that so outdistances the pack over a short time frame will be able to maintain that pace for the long term. Is there not an inherent contradiction in featuring short-term performance in a process (investing) that by definition is long term in nature? A baseball player may go 4-4 in one game, but no one has batted 1.000 for a season. (Actually, players now command multimillion dollar salaries simply by batting .300.)

To cure yourself of any lingering susceptibility you might have towards hare funds, do the following calculations. The next time you see one of these novas featured for spectacular performance over a matter of months, multiply their performance out to an annual number (up 20% for six months would equal a 40% return for a full year). Then multiply that result out for three and five years (40% annually would equal a cumulative 120% for three years and 200% for five years). Finally, study one of the available mutual fund statistical services to see if any funds have achieved such lofty levels in recent three- or five-year time frames. Let me save you the trouble. You probably will not find any. To use a piece of modern investment science technology: there is no correlation between most funds' performance over the short term and the long term.

Assuming we are agreed that a portfolio of tortoises is preferable to a conglomeration of hares (even if they have high correlation coefficients), let us in a general sense explore the notion of a tortoise portfolio. How to actually put such a portfolio together will be described in detail later. As long as we are onto sports analogies, let's use one more.

The investor is the equal of a football coach. His job is to develop an overall strategy (investment objective) and a game plan (active asset allocation). It is up to the players (funds) to execute this game plan. The coach prefers consistent players (tortoises), those that will deliver whether the team is playing at home (bull markets) or on the road (bear markets). He will never try to anticipate who will perform above the norm in any game setting, so he will place equal emphasis (equal dollar weighting) on all his players (funds). As long as the majority perform up to expectations (median-plus returns) each game (segment of market cycle), while the rest perform reasonably well (near median, none in the 70th, 80th, or 90th percentiles), the team will likely have a winning season (achieve the desired objective).

That's the basis of tortoise investing. That is why it is so important to define the guidelines by which funds are categorized as tortoises—which is what we will explore next.

5

IN SEARCH OF TORTOISES

BESIDES THE attraction to novas, perhaps the single most common trap into which investors fall is the belief that mutual fund selection does not require homework. Isn't that why you chose mutual funds in lieu of stocks and bonds in the first place? You didn't have the time, expertise, or determination to investigate the merits of individual issues, so you handed over responsibility to a mutual fund manager.

The fund industry itself is quite culpable in this regard. We live in an age of "instant gratification," and the industry has positioned itself as an "instant" investment option. Don't have the time or training for equity and debt selection? Presto, here's the XYZ fund to do it all for you! Many an investor has fallen prey to just that hype. This fund can afford a full-page ad in the Sunday business section of my newspaper; they must be a solid choice.

Boys and girls, there are now more stock and bond mutual funds than there are New York Stock Exchange–listed issues. Judging the suitability of a particular fund by the size of its ads, by the glossiness of its marketing materials, by an article in the financial press, or by a recommendation in an advisory letter, simply will not suffice. You would not (I hope) buy a stock or bond unless some analyst had performed in-depth research. You would not invest in a piece of real estate or an oil or gas property before a qualified individual or firm had undertaken the requisite due diligence. Is an investment in a mutual fund any less serious? Does it not require the same level of due diligence?

That's the bad news—there is no instant approach to fund selection. The good news—if you follow the systematic approach I am about to share with you, it will *not* be anywhere near as time consuming as you might first guess. Why? *Because there simply are not that many tortoise funds.* They are proverbial needles in a haystack, and I will give you a simple three-step process to ferret them out. Conversely, the vast majority of funds do *not* belong in your portfolio; over 95 percent of the total universe will normally be ruled out of consideration. A veritable handful will make it through our screens.

I mentioned in passing the shortcomings of selecting funds via advisory letters. To be kind, the advisory letter field is a virtual wasteland. My standard response when asked whether I subscribe to such letters is "Yes, but only because the Sunday *New York Times* does not have a comics section!" It is laughable what passes as advice. Many of these sheets simply recommend what is currently hot ("The Hare Syndrome"); others concoct the most outrageous selection methodologies.

Three stand out. One suggests always being invested in the ten best performing funds over the past few months. As funds fall out of the top ten, you will sell them and buy their replacements on the list. In other words, sell funds as their performance falls off a cliff and buy those whose performance may be approaching a peak. How's that for brilliance!

The second purports to provide buy points and sell points for a select group of funds. How ridiculous! In the first place, funds are in great measure dependent on market action (growth funds rarely rise in value in a declining market). If the market is declining, you will likely hit the buy point on most, if not all, growth funds simultaneously. Do you want to be buying into growth funds when the market may be in the early stages of a major decline? Second, the idea of buy points and sell points equates to an investment becoming undervalued or overvalued. How, I ask you, how can an open-ended fund that is constantly shuffling the mix of stocks and/or bonds in its portfolio become over- or undervalued unless you make a moment-to-moment assessment of each and every security in its portfolio?

The third one literally tops them all (I believe it currently has the widest circulation of all these letters). Follow along: track how each fund performed in relation to the overall market this past year. Then make a forecast about how the market will perform this coming year, and with a simple wave of the wand you know how your fund will do. For instance, if the market is up 10 percent in 1990 and Fund A rose 15 percent. If you forecast that the market will advance 20 percent in 1991, then it follows that Fund A will be up 30 percent.

I'll give you a moment to dry the tears of laughter out of your eyes. When they coined the phrase, "There oughtta be a law," I think they had these quacks in mind. But there is no law; anyone can become an advisory letter publisher without any qualifications. And that is the sad part, because of all the unknowing, trusting souls who get duped. No need to do research and come up with some solid tortoise funds, Mr. Novice Investor. I'll give you some instant winners. Just buy my letter.

No, there are no shortcuts. You must do research, apply some due diligence. Instant investing will lead to instant disaster. You must invest the time. If you feel you don't have the time, don't get started in the first place. All you will accomplish is to create some future tax losses for yourself.

There is another positive aspect to the search for tortoises. Once identified, your list will remain fairly intact for long periods of time. You've heard of a leopard not changing its spots; well, we can now add to that, "Once a tortoise, always a tortoise." Every rule has its exception, and a bit later I will define the sell discipline for tortoise funds. But for the most part, if you do it right the first time, turnover in your "approved list" will be surprisingly low. (Unlike many lists of favored funds now appearing in business magazines. Examine the changes in their lists from year to year, and you will note average annual turnover of 25–33 percent. Not a very convincing affirmation of their selection methodology.)

6

THE THREE P'S

THE SEARCH for tortoise funds is a three-stage process that step by step will winnow out the few funds suitable for our portfolio. If there is a common thread running through each stage it is *consistency*. I have already raised this idea in the last chapter, and it is one that will arise over and over again throughout the remainder of the book. When I am asked to describe funds that I favor, it is the term I use most often. Let's identify the three stages: performance, people, and process.

PERFORMANCE

Ours is a non-traditional approach to performance analysis. While many are attracted to leaders, we are inclined to look further down the list—not necessarily at the laggards, but, shall we say, more towards the middle of the pack. Our interest is in finding funds with sustained consistency;

rarely if ever do you find such funds at the top of perform-ance charts (except when looking at long periods of time, generally ten years or more). As we suggested in the last chapter, lists of leaders over short time frames are dotted with funds displaying short-term brilliance. They are highly susceptible to burnout.

Tortoise-style funds, on the other hand, in stressing con-sistency, rarely gravitate to the top. Where do you find them? Experience has shown they are most apt to be linger-ing in the second quartile. If you divide up the fund uni-verse into four quartiles ranked by performance, the leaders would be in the top quartile, and the laggards in the bottom quartile. Tortoises generally deliver median-plus type returns, or somewhere in the 26th to 50th percentile. In a good year, they inch into the top quartile; in a "bad" year, somewhat below the midpoint.

Under normal conditions, this test can be run against the total fund universe. However, under special circum-stances, they may have to be run by peer groups. For in-stance, after a sustained rise in the stock market it will be difficult to find bond funds ranked in the top half. Yet even mediocre equity managers get dragged into the top half of the universe during a sustained bull market in stocks. The result: even good bond managers find it difficult to forge above the 50th percentile.

Warning No. 1: Don't Try to Cut Corners and Save Time by Studying Cumulative Performance Results

You *must* look at the year-by-year record. Let me show you why.

Compare the three-year cumulative record of two funds (Table 6.1) and they appear as equals. Study the year-by-year record, and it's a completely different story. Literally night and day. The hare does 2½ times as well as the tor-toise in Year 1 and twice as well in Year 3 (care to guess who was featured in the quarterly, semiannual and annual mutual-fund roundups in the financial press during those

TABLE 6.1

Cumulative Performance: The Tortoise vs. the Hare

	Hare	Tortoise
Year 1	+50%	+20%
Year 2	−20	+15
Year 3	+33	+16
Total	+60%	+60%

two years?). But look closely at Year 2. The hare stopped for a rest.

True, if you had the good fortune to invest in the hare just prior to Year 1, three years later you made out as well as if you had invested in the tortoise. However, three questions must be answered: (1) Was the end result worth the roller-coaster–induced aggravation of the year-to-year ups and downs? (2) What if you were forced to liquidate after Year 2? Hare: +20% (plus aggravation), Tortoise: +38%! (3) What if you were attracted to the hare by a feature story appearing after its spectacular performance in Year 1, and first invested at the beginning of Year 2; how did you do over the remaining two years? Hare: +6.4%, Tortoise: 33.4% (remember the Risk of Losses).

The bottom line: Over the three years, the hare does as well as the tortoise, but leaves you with many a sleepless night. Over the first two years, the tortoise does almost twice as well; over the last two, over five times better. Moral: *Don't be fooled by cumulative returns. Stay away from hares.* You win by not losing.

Warning No. 2: To Reiterate, Do Not Be Attracted to Hyper-Performance over the Short Term

Take a lesson from what happens to moths attracted to flames, except note that in the case of mutual funds it's worse because these flames quickly die out. There are two ways to reinforce this point. One, how long do top performers remain at the top of the list. Two, how did outstanding performers over the long term get the 2? How did they do year by year?

As they say, the proof is in the pudding (Table 6.2). Clearly, this is not a one- or two-year phenomenon. Time and again, and we have covered an extended period here representing many different market environments, buying today's winner looks no better than a 50:50 bet whether you will own tomorrow's winner or loser. Here we see *no* consistency at all between current performance and future performance (or as the investment scientists would put it—very low R-squares). The regulators are absolutely correct in demanding that fund sales literature include the disclaimer: "Past performance is no guarantee of future performance." How true, how true.

Here is the flip-side of the story. When a moment ago we studied one-year top performers, the evidence was clear: *Hares have no staying power.* Table 6.3 presents the converse: *Tortoises deliver over the longer term, rarely over the shorter term.*

Remember, investing is a long-term process. If you are in it for the long term, what difference does it make how your choices do over the short term? This is particularly so when we look at the cream of long-term performers. Unlike the hares, who often fall from the heights to the very depths, long-term tortoises present a completely different picture. When these consistent funds falter, it is generally into the third quartile, or slightly below average. Outright disasters are rare to them.

This view is further reinforced by a study performed by Wyatt Associates, a leading benefits consulting organization. Investment managers (as well as fund managers) are more likely to fall to the back of the pack from the front than from the middle (Table 6.4). And, again, since *(a)* we are most concerned about long-term results, and *(b)* we want to stay away from the Risk of Losses (i.e., back-of-the-pack performance), then it follows *(c)* we should focus our selection process on middle-of-the-pack funds. Middle of the pack = tortoises.

Warning No. 3: Beware of the Fund du Jour

If there is one thing the fund industry is not lacking, it is marketing creativity. "Sell them what they want, not what they need." They are always there at the ready for what will sell at the moment. And that moment normally marks the beginning of the end. In the early 80s technology was the hot topic. Presto, dozens of technology funds, most of which were launched within twelve months of the top in high-tech valuations.

Short-term interest rates got you down? Shazam! Dozens of government-plus funds appear. Depressed over the shambles in the junk bond area? May I show you our new "prime rate trust"? (This vehicle bears as much resemblance to a mutual fund as the bride of Frankenstein bore to a woman. No liquidity to speak of, false valuations, etc. Sold as a quasi–money-market fund, but much more quasi than fund.)

The hype for each of these flavors of the week is basically the same. "A once-in-a-lifetime opportunity." "Brand new." "The chance to get in on the ground floor." Forget it, it's all drivel. I'll repeat: you invest for the long term. Therefore, when selecting specific investments, you should have in mind holding them five-to-ten years or longer. Since that's the case, you *don't* want to purchase something that is brand new; you *don't* want to get in on the ground floor.

Let someone else be the guinea pig. Wait one, two, or three years; if this new-fangled flavor of the month is for real, it will work for a great deal longer than the time you waited to check it out. (And don't be swayed by the arguments of the promoters that their idea has been "back-tested" for five, ten, or twenty years. Poppycock! Everything works great on the computer. Portfolio insurance worked great in every simulation, in every professor's

TABLE 6.2
Yearly Top Ten Performers

TOP TEN FUNDS
WHERE DID THEY RANK IN THE YEARS WHICH FOLLOWED?

	1982	1983	1984	1985	1986	1987	1988	1989	1990
OPPENHEIMER TARGET	1	136	606	216	779	1160	25	768	825
LOOMIS SAYLES CAPITAL	2	318	529	22	75	71	1386	788	600
NEW ENGLAND GROWTH FUND	3	418	506	90	228	59	1368	594	462
UNITED SERVICES GOLD SHARES	4	563	639	767	47	26	1463	2	1701
STRATEGIC INVESTMENTS	5	573	645	768	74	40	1464	3	1707
IDS PROGRESSIVE	6	265	465	164	725	562	199	1304	1585
FIDELITY SEL. TECH	7	3	602	740	931	1123	1402	847	59
PUTNAM VISTA	8	329	554	250	188	307	480	414	1162
MASS FIN EMERGING GROWTH	9	50	514	360	549	1099	477	412	1383
FIDELITY PRECIOUS METALS	10	599	632	759	55	17	1461	175	1631
OPPENHEIMER REGENCY		1	624	159	785	541	712	618	1114
JANA GROWTH		2	Fund is not traceable, and it may no longer exist.						59
FIDELITY SEL. TECH		3	602	740	931	1123	1402	847	877
ALLIANCE TECHNOLOGY		4	601	341	596	55	1378	1528	1413
FIRST INV. DISCOVERY		5	643	684	939	1167	374	88	550
STRONG INVESMENT		6	175	582	265	755	846	1281	1127
LINDNER DIVIDEND		7	34	635	160	944	104	1211	1466
ROYCE VALUE FUND		8	382	287	821	694	110	894	1568
LEGG MASON VALUE TRUST		9	84	155	745	1036	83	679	1163
STRONG TOTAL RETURN		10	159	376	176	237	435	1585	

	Fund						
1	PRU–BACHE UTIL.	117	59	1066	132	95	1123
2	VANGUARD HIGH YIELD STOCK	207	138	971	76	1582	1693
3	COPLEY FUND	387	271	1057	225	795	781
4	SLH AMER. TELECOMM	122	95	654	341	10	803
5	FRANKLIN UTIL.	462	108	994	678	408	669
6	ENERGY & UTILITY SHARES	212	388	1114	817	742	946
7	FIDELITY SEL. UTIL.	157	104	1083	381	67	658
8	FIDELITY QUAL. DVD.	368	154	952	790	704	657
9	WINDSOR FUND	268	169	623	52	941	1522
10	SEQUOIA FUND	274	508	197	713	317	944
1	FIDELITY OVERSEAS	1	7	60	931	848	1134
2	FIDELITY OTC	2	636	592	128	234	1010
3	NEW ENG ZENITH CAP GRWTH	3	1	4	1434	221	*
4	PAINE WEBBER ATLAS	4	44	333	219	678	1180
5	PUTNAM INTL EQUITIES	5	48	165	867	474	1282
6	ALLIANCE INTL	6	33	988	23	257	1630
7	FT INTL	7	14	749	400	767	1388
8	HEMISPHERE FUND	8	290	706	293	276	1217
9	FIDELITY SEL. HEALTH	9	136	780	881	42	5
10	GAM INTL	10	26	103	376	582	1178
1	NEW ENG ZENITH CAP GRWTH		1	4	1434	221	*
2	MERRILL LYNCH PACIFIC		2	87	38	870	1283
3	NOMURA PACIFIC BASIN		3	20	387	574	1518
4	TYNDALL–NEWPORT FAR EAST		4	527	542	1296	1360
5	FINANCIAL POST–PACIFIC		5	138	119	680	1665

TABLE 6.2 (Continued)

TOP TEN FUNDS
WHERE DID THEY RANK IN THE YEARS WHICH FOLLOWED?

	1982	1983	1984	1985	1986	1987	1988	1989	1990
GT PACIFIC GROWTH FUND					6	465	118	20	1363
FIDELITY OVERSEAS					7	60	931	848	1134
BBK INTL					8	435	666	1020	1609
T. ROWE PRICE INTL					9	176	305	508	1267
GT JAPAN GROWTH					10	6	161	4	1689
OPPENHEIMER NINETY – TEN						1	1418	1548	859
DFA JAPAN SMALL COMPANY						2	27	73	1700
OPPENHEIMER GLD & SP MIN.						3	919	127	1680
NEW ENG ZENITH CAP GRWTH						4	1434	221	*
IDS PRECIOUS METALS						5	1447	806	1657
GT JAPAN GROWTH						6	161	4	1689
DFA UNITED KINGDOM SM. CO.						7	847	1662	1136
FRANKLIN GOLD FUND						8	1438	46	1615
VAN ECK GOLD/RESOURCES						9	1459	739	1677
COLONIAL ADV. STR. GOLD						10	1440	1108	1678
KAUFMANN FUND							1	22	1094
INTERGRATED EQ. AGG. GROWTH							2	544	1681
PARNASSUS FUND							3	1583	1635
COLUMBIA SPECIAL							4	183	1422

CALVERT ARIEL GROWTH	5	446	1543
GABELLI GROWTH	6	60	818
FIDELITY SEL. RETAIL	7	258	1026
FIDELITY SEL. TRANS.	8	296	1639
HARBOR INTERN. FUND	9	98	1308
FIDELITY CAPITAL APPR.	10	360	1527

ALGER: SMALL CAPITAL	1	389
US GOLD SHARES	2	1701
STRATEGIC INVESTMENTS	3	1707
GT GLBL GROWTH: JAPAN	4	1689
FINANCIAL PORT: HEALTH	5	4
FIDELITY SEL. ENERGY SER.	6	591
FIDELITY SEL. MEDICAL	7	23
VISTA FDS: GROWTH & INCOME	8	678
GT GLOBAL GROWTH: AMERICA	9	1185
SLH AMER. TELECOMM: INC.	10	803

* New England Zenith Capital Growth is no longer categorized as a mutual fund for comparisons by Lipper Analytical Services but is categorized as variable annuity and variable life.

TABLE 6.3

Top 25 Funds from 12/31/80 to 12/31/90 with Rankings for Each Year

TOP 25 FUNDS FROM 12/31/80 TO 12/31/90 WITH RANKINGS FOR EACH YEAR FROM 1981 TO 1990

Top 25 Performers	Ten Years 12/31/80– 12/31/90	1990	1989	1988	1987	1986	1985	1984	1983	1982	1981
Fidelity Magellan Fund	1	988	128	132	647	107	33	338	17	16	19
Merrill Pacific; A	2	1281	870	39	86	2	41	313	19	511	7
Phoenix Growth Fund	3	425	337	1093	121	204	156	165	73	33	235
CGM Capital Development (1)	4	600	788	1390	72	75	22	529	318	2	185
Sequoia Fund	5	943	317	725	199	508	274	10	86	158	8
Fidelity Destiny I	6	888	419	250	249	227	239	283	21	57	94
Quest for Value Fund	7	1152	689	320	865	455	298	294	15	41	3
Japan Fund (2)	8	1549	1234	241	25	n/a	n/a	n/a	n/a	n/a	n/a
Oppenheimer Target	9	825	768	25	1165	779	216	606	136	1	1
Lindner Dividend (3)	10	1127	1211	104	948	160	635	34	7	170	4
FPA Paramount (4)	11	595	566	227	44	844	592	167	44	20	n/a
United: Income	12	1057	335	223	204	131	107	246	43	153	218
Washington Mutual Inv	13	945	281	318	610	120	152	196	103	96	91
New Eng: Growth Fund (5)	14	462	594	1372	59	228	90	506	418	3	205
Mutual: Qualified	15	1328	979	31	193	296	367	21	29	430	6
Lindner Fund	16	1376	632	207	161	470	579	83	134	260	2
Phoenix: Balanced Fd	17	343	454	1343	140	190	213	60	264	48	172
Sogen International	18	766	833	502	85	92	132	326	131	167	78
Franklin Cust: Utilities	19	669	408	677	997	108	462	5	310	150	9

Investment Co of America	20	648	265	566	291	150	115	242	209	111	259
Twentieth Cent: Select	21	719	64	1237	262	164	109	524	56	34	247
Janus Fund	22	734	23	374	352	653	394	381	109	169	97
IDS New Dimensions	23	454	190	951	78	207	78	470	216	109	272
Windsor Fds: Windsor	24	1521	941	52	628	169	268	9	51	354	18
New York Venture	25	867	126	171	825	134	61	289	164	291	251

(1) formerly Loomis-Sayles Capital Development changed in 1990
to the current name CGM = Capital Growth Management
(2) Japan Fund was a closed-end fund up to 1987
when it was purchased by Scudder, Stevens and Clark
(3) formerly Lindner Fund for Income
(4) formerly Paramount Fund
(5) formerly NEL Growth (New England Life)
Source: Lipper Analytical Services, Inc.

TABLE 6.4

Performance Bracket Changes, 1985–1989

Number of Brackets Moved	Upgraded				No Change	Downgraded				Drop Outs
	+4	+3	+2	+1		−1	−2	−3	−4	
1980–84 Classification:										
Super	*	*	*	*	0%	3%	13%	35%	37%	12%
High	*	*	*	3%	3%	23%	41%	18%	*	13%
Market	*	*	0%	2%	17%	34%	31%	*	*	16%
Substandard	*	0%	1%	11%	38%	34%	*	*	*	16%
Poor	0%	0%	8%	28%	48%	*	*	*	*	16%

*Not possible
Source: Wyatt Asset Services, Inc., 1990

computer, in every back-tested historical period. It only failed in one place—the real world.)

In short, the fund industry excels at appealing to investors' worst instincts. Don't be fooled!

Warning No. 4: Don't Buy Sector Funds

In many ways, these are the low point of the fund industry. Why does one purchase a mutual fund? Because you want a full-time professional to make all portfolio decisions for you. In return for which, you are willing to pay an investment advisory fee. By comparison, in a sector fund you continue to pay the fee to the manager, but *you* perform the more critical task—selecting industry groups.

Let me explain: in terms of what has the *greatest* impact on your ultimate portfolio returns, the most critical decision you make is whether to be in stocks or not and in what proportion to your total investable assets, a.k.a., asset allocation. Second most critical decision—industry selection. Third—individual stock selection. But by purchasing sector funds, you make the second most critical decision and the fund manager the third. If there were any justice in this world, the fund manager should be paying the advisory fee to you!

Think about it: would you rather own the best performing stock in the worst performing industry group (the best of the worst) or the worst performing stock in the best performing industry group? In other words, if your industry selection skills leave something to be desired, however talented the manager of your selected sector fund, its returns will probably leave you underwater. The thing that confuses me is why an individual feels qualified to select industry groups but not individual stocks. Simply to save time? A very poor excuse.

When I am asked whether I buy sector funds, I answer, "Yes. But I call them growth funds. In a growth fund, I'm investing in sectors, but instead of my having to select them, I leave it up to a full-time professional qualified for the task." It's that simple: *if you believe in the validity of sector funds, buy a well-managed growth fund.*

Enough negatives. Let's switch gears and look at some positives. And the most noteworthy of all positives is this: *there are very few tortoise funds.* Many potential fund investors feel overwhelmed when they discover that there are now more open-ended stock and bond mutual funds than there are New York Stock Exchange–listed issues. Don't despair! The methodology I will share with you in a moment will generally knock out 90 percent, plus or minus, of all funds from consideration.

Remember, the key word is consistency. And very, very few funds deliver consistent performance. How do you define consistency? There are a number of different ways, but to keep it simple let's use the following screen. In order to qualify as a tortoise fund, a candidate must have ranked in the top half of the fund universe in each of the last three years. Three years is a long enough period of time to discern if a fund has staying power (in other words, long enough to weed out the Fund du Jours and the one-shot flashes). It is not so long that it will knock out every candidate; remember that even tortoises rest every once in a while. If you were to screen for top-half rankings for somewhere between five and seven years, there wouldn't be enough survivors from which to compose our portfolio.

How many tortoises do we find in a three-year test? Table 6.5 shows 110 funds whose names begin with the letter "A" as of 31 December 1990. Using the years 1990, 1989 and 1988 as a measurement period, we see only 6 funds, or 6 percent, that qualify as tortoises. Had we examined the entire fund universe approximately the same proportion would have held.

To repeat, there are very few tortoises. Rather than having to investigate in depth over 1500 funds, our first screen alone has reduced the candidates list to no more than 100 to 150. That is a manageable total! The second positive is that the next of our three "P's" will narrow down the field even further.

PEOPLE

Not to be facetious, but mutual funds do not run themselves. Nor, for that matter, do computers. People run mutual funds, and without having a handle on those people, in reality one knows very little about that fund.

It is curious that as I write this the fund industry is once again fighting vehemently to squash a Securities and Exchange Commission (SEC) proposal that would require fund prospectuses to list the name of the portfolio manager of that fund. This proposal has been brought up a number of times, and each time industry forces have successfully killed it. Their argument is that a fund has a specific investment style, and whether Mr. Smith or Mr. Jones is the manager is immaterial.

Rubbish! You do not need more than your ten fingers to count the number of funds with an exemplary performance record that have continued to perform well after a manager change. There are exceptions, of course, but for the most part *the manager makes the fund, not vice versa.*

An analogy would be a sailing regatta in which each sailor is assigned a similar vessel. Yet one competitor will consistently outperform his or her rivals. Why? Because their boat was superior? No, each competitor had similar equipment. What separated this individual from the others was talent and the crew. So it is in the mutual fund business. You have to know the captain and his or her crew.

(Pardon my cynicism, but if the industry would have us believe that the fund is more important than the individual, why then are so many fund groups offering baseball-size employment contracts to managers they are attempting to pirate away from other fund groups?)

TABLE 6.5

CDA Monthly Alphabetic Listing, 12/31/90

FUND	MGT CO	IO	ASSETS MIL$	NAV	MAX LOAD	% DIVD	ANNUALIZED ROR THRU 12/31/90					
							10 YEARS		5 YEARS		3 YEARS	
							PCNT	RK	PCNT	RK	PCNT	RK
AAL CAPITAL GROWTH FD	AALA	G	141	11.06	4.8	2.3	na	—	na	—	13.6	10
AAL INCOME FUND	AALA	BPC	110	9.66	4.8	7.7	na	—	na	—	9.2	48
AARP CAPITAL GROWTH	SCUDER	AG	160	23.57	0.0	2.3	na	—	10.6	22	12.6	14
AARP GNMA/US TREAS FD	SCUDER	BPG	2583	15.28	0.0	8.5	na	—	8.5	52	9.5	42
AARP GROWTH AND INCOME	SCUDER	GI	248	23.45	0.0	5.2	na	—	10.6	23	11.2	21
AARP HIGH QUALITY BOND	SCUDER	BPC	151	15.12	0.0	7.7	na	—	8.2	57	9.3	46
AARP INSD TXFR GEN BOND	SCUDER	MB	766	16.68	0.0	6.2	na	—	9.0	43	9.8	38
AARP INSD TXFR SH-TERM	SCUDER	MB	98	15.20	0.0	6.2	na	—	5.8	83	5.6	83
ABT EMERGING GROWTH	PBCM	AG	15	7.89	4.8	0.0	na	—	6.2	80	12.6	14
ABT GROWTH & INCOME TR.	PBCM	G	79	8.42	4.8	3.7	8.9	81	8.6	50	7.6	72
ABT SECURITY INCOME	PBCM	GI	5	9.22	4.8	4.3	na	—	3.5	90	9.0	51
ABT UTILITY INCOME FD	PBCM	GIS	133	11.56	4.8	5.5	10.8	61	10.6	23	13.3	11
ACORN FUND	HARRIS	G	738	32.57	0.0*	1.9	11.3	52	9.2	40	8.6	59
ADDISON CAPITAL SHARES	ADDCAP	G	25	16.60	3.0	1.6	na	—	na	—	10.4	29
ADTEK FUND	HEATH	GI	7	9.35	0.0	1.7	na	—	3.8	90	3.0	88
ADVEST ADVANTAGE GOVT	BOSTON	BPG	107	8.47	0.0*	8.1	na	—	na	—	7.7	70
ADVEST ADVANTAGE GROWTH	BOSTON	G	25	12.49	0.0*	0.9	na	—	na	—	9.7	38
ADVEST ADVANTAGE INCOME	BOSTON	B	45	10.13	0.0*	6.4	na	—	na	—	10.4	28
ADVEST ADVANTAGE SPECIAL	BOSTON	AG	3	10.67	0.0*	0.0	na	—	na	—	10.5	26
AEGON USA CAPITAL APPREC	AEGON	GI	9	3.05	5.8	2.7	8.5	84	5.8	83	4.0	86
AEGON USA GROWTH PORTF	AEGON	GI	32	5.03	5.8	3.7	10.9	60	7.7	67	6.2	81
AEGON USA HIYLD PORTF	AEGON	BPH	33	9.23	5.5	10.7	na	—	8.1	60	8.7	58
AFFILIATED FUND	LD-ABT	GI	3047	8.95	6.8*	4.2	13.5	23	10.9	20	9.6	41
AFUTURE FUND	CARLIL	G	7	8.88	0.0	2.1	1.6	97	-3.2	98	0.6	92
AGE HIGH INCOME FUND	FRNKRE	BPH	1416	2.01	4.0	19.1	8.4	84	1.6	94	-1.9	95
AIM CHARTER FUND	AIM	G	99	6.58	5.5	2.1	12.7	32	14.9	5	15.7	5
AIM CONSTELLATION FUND	AIM	AG	83	7.73	5.5	0.0	10.1	72	15.2	5	13.6	6
AIM CONVERTIBLE SECS INC	AIM	G	10	9.52	4.8	3.0	6.1	91	2.3	93	6.9	76
AIM HIGH YLD SECURITIES	AIM	BPH	39	4.95	4.8	16.8	7.1	88	-0.9	96	-5.2	97
AIM LIMITED MATURITY	AIM	BPG	80	9.90	1.8	7.5	na	—	na	—	8.3	64
AIM SUMMIT FUND	AIM	AG	275	7.56	5.5	1.9	na	—	11.0	20	15.8	5
AIM WEINGARTEN FUND	AIM	G	597	12.14	5.5	0.7	15.1	9	16.8	3	16.9	3
ALGER SMALL CAP PORTF	ALGER	AG	23	15.28	0.0*	0.0	na	—	na	—	27.0	1
ALLIANCE BALANCED SHARES	ALLIAN	B	141	11.24	5.5*	3.4	13.6	21	9.1	41	9.0	50
ALLIANCE BD-MTHLY INCOME	ALLIAN	BPC	67	11.32	5.5	10.2	12.8	31	8.6	51	8.9	53
ALLIANCE BD-US GOVT	ALLIAN	BPG	494	8.17	5.5	9.7	na	—	8.1	61	8.9	52
ALLIANCE CONVERTIBLE	ALLIAN	GI	39	6.78	5.5*	6.5	na	—	na	—	-0.2	93
ALLIANCE COUNTERPOINT FD	ALLIAN	G	49	16.00	5.5	1.3	na	—	12.7	12	15.2	6
ALLIANCE FUND	ALLIAN	AG	572	5.22	5.5	3.0	10.0	72	10.4	25	11.9	18
ALLIANCE GLOBAL-CANADIAN	ALLIAN	ING	23	5.61	5.5	0.0	8.0	87	7.8	65	8.5	61
ALLIANCE GLOBL SM CAP A	ALLIAN	AG	68	8.51	5.5	0.0	6.5	90	5.8	82	6.4	80
ALLIANCE GROWTH & INCOME	ALLIAN	G	319	2.17	5.5	3.7	14.1	16	11.9	15	12.7	14
ALLIANCE HIGH YIELD BOND	ALLIAN	BPH	104	4.60	5.5	14.5	na	—	-2.3	97	-6.6	98
ALLIANCE INTERNATIONAL A	ALLIAN	INF	217	13.88	5.5	0.2	na	—	13.0	11	10.8	25
ALLIANCE MORTGAGE SECS	ALLIAN	BPG	509	8.79	5.5	9.4	na	—	9.0	43	10.2	30
ALLIANCE MUNI INCOME-CA	ALLIAN	MB	139	9.69	4.5	6.7	na	—	na	—	10.3	29
ALLIANCE MUNI INCOME-NAT	ALLIAN	MB	183	9.62	4.5	6.7	na	—	na	—	10.8	25
ALLIANCE MUNI INCOME-NY	ALLIAN	MB	118	8.95	4.5*	6.8	na	—	na	—	9.9	35
ALLIANCE MUNI INSD CA	ALLIAN	MB	56	12.44	4.5	6.0	na	—	8.0	63	9.5	41

TABLE 6.5 *(Continued)*

FUND	MGT CO	IO	ASSETS MIL$	NAV	MAX LOAD	% DIVD	ANNUALIZED ROR THRU 12/31/90					
							10 YEARS		5 YEARS		3 YEARS	
							PCNT	RK	PCNT	RK	PCNT	RK
ALLIANCE MUNI INSD NATL	ALLIAN	MB	116	9.53	4.5*	6.2	na	—	na	—	9.9	36
ALLIANCE QUASAR	ALLIAN	AG	251	16.15	5.5	0.4	11.1	56	6.1	81	8.4	62
ALLIANCE SH-TERM MULTI A	ALLIAN	BPI	1226	9.82	3.0	10.7	na	—	na	—	na	—
ALLIANCE SH-TERM MULTI B	ALLIAN	BPI	1772	9.82	0.0*	na	na	—	na	—	na	—
ALLIANCE TECHNOLOGY	ALLIAN	AG	112	19.44	5.5	0.0	na	—	6.7	77	1.3	91
ALPINE CALIF MUNI ASSET	ALPINE	MB	24	10.00	3.8	6.9	na	—	na	—	na	—
ALPINE NATL MUNI ASSET	ALPINE	MB	6	9.35	3.8	6.7	na	—	na	—	5.7	82
AMA GLOBAL INCOME FD	AMA	BPI	16	19.24	0.0	10.0	na	—	na	—	6.9	77
AMA GROWTH-CLASSIC PORTF	AMA	G	24	7.40	0.0	2.7	6.9	89	4.8	88	5.0	84
AMA GROWTH-GLOBAL PORTF	AMA	ING	90	19.70	0.0	3.0	na	—	na	—	8.7	56
AMA GROWTH-GROW PLUS INC	AMA	GI	8	10.00	0.0	2.2	na	—	na	—	6.5	79
AMA USG INCOME PLUS	AMA	BPG	40	8.57	0.0	8.3	10.4	68	7.0	75	7.7	70
AMCAP FUND	CAPRES	G	1679	9.97	5.8	2.3	13.0	28	11.3	18	9.8	37
AMERICAN BALANCED FUND	CAPRES	B	327	10.32	3.8	5.7	13.7	20	10.3	26	10.4	27
AMERICAN CAP COMSTOCK	AM-CAP	G	770	14.29	8.5	3.0	13.7	19	10.4	25	13.1	13
AMERICAN CAP CORP BOND	AM-CAP	BPC	189	6.38	4.8	9.7	12.2	39	8.5	52	8.4	63
AMERICAN CAP EMERGING GR	AM-CAP	G	189	14.67	5.8	0.5	11.7	47	8.1	59	10.9	24
AMERICAN CAP ENTERPRISE	AM-CAP	G	503	10.76	5.8	2.0	9.2	78	9.7	32	12.5	15
AMERICAN CAP EQUITY INC	AM-CAP	B	82	4.00	5.8	5.5	13.6	21	8.3	56	9.3	46
AMERICAN CAP GR & INCOME	AM-CAP	G	136	10.09	5.8	3.2	12.2	38	8.1	60	8.4	63
AMERICAN CAPITAL FED MTG	AM-CAP	BPG	32	12.85	4.8	8.7	na	—	na	—	9.4	44
AMERICAN CAPITAL GOV SEC	AM-CAP	BPG	3902	10.27	4.8	8.6	na	—	7.7	66	10.1	33
AMERICAN CAPITAL HARBOR	AM-CAP	B	331	12.93	5.8	6.3	12.0	42	8.7	49	11.6	19
AMERICAN CAPITAL HIYLD	AM-CAP	BPH	299	4.82	4.8	18.0	7.1	88	-1.7	95	-5.5	97
AMERICAN CAPITAL MUNI BD	AM-CAP	MB	236	18.74	4.8	6.1	10.9	59	7.7	67	10.0	34
AMERICAN CAPITAL PACE FD	AM-CAP	G	2047	10.84	5.8	2.4	14.5	14	8.8	48	10.6	26
AMERICAN CAPITAL TXF HIY	AM-CAP	MB	221	10.66	4.8	7.6	na	—	na	—	7.8	69
AMERICAN CAPITAL TXF INS	AM-CAP	MB	40	10.88	4.8	6.5	na	—	na	—	8.3	64
AMERICAN FDS-TX EX CALIF	CAPRES	MB	87	14.35	4.8	5.6	na	—	na	—	8.0	67
AMERICAN FDS-TX EX MD	CAPRES	MB	31	14.19	4.8	5.6	na	—	na	—	8.4	62
AMERICAN FDS-TX EX VA	CAPRES	MB	33	14.45	4.8	5.8	na	—	na	—	7.8	69
AMERICAN GAS INDEX	RUSH	G	107	10.24	0.0	5.3	na	—	na	—	na	—
AMERICAN GROWTH FUND	INVSMT	GI	64	7.02	8.5	3.4	9.3	77	6.7	77	8.0	67
AMERICAN HERITAGE FUND	HERTGE	AG	1	0.72	0.0	0.0	-9.8	99	-14.6	99	-9.1	98
AMERICAN HIGH-INC TR	CAPRES	BPH	140	11.72	4.8	12.9	na	—	na	—	na	—
AMERICAN INVESTORS GR FD	AM-INV	AG	62	5.79	8.5	0.5	-1.7	97	4.6	88	9.3	46
AMERICAN INVS INCOME	AM-INV	BPH	9	4.70	5.0	13.1	3.7	95	-1.3	97	-6.1	98
AMERICAN LEADERS FUND	FEDLIB	GI	124	11.34	4.5	3.5	13.3	25	7.1	74	7.1	75
AMERICAN MUTUAL FUND	CAPRES	GI	3200	18.67	5.8	4.9	15.2	8	11.5	17	11.6	19
AMERICAN NATIONAL GROWTH	SECRES	GI	91	3.95	8.5	2.0	12.2	39	9.9	29	8.5	59
AMERICAN NATL INC FUND	SECRES	GI	68	19.35	8.5	3.8	14.0	17	9.5	35	12.0	17
AMERICAN PERF BOND FUND	BANCOK	BPC	40	10.41	4.0	na	na	—	na	—	na	—
AMERICAN PERF EQUITY FD	BANCOK	G	40	10.37	4.0	na	na	—	na	—	na	—
AMERICAN PERF INTERM BD	BANCOK	BPC	25	10.27	4.0	na	na	—	na	—	na	—
AMEV ADVANTAGE-ASSET ALL	AMEV	B	21	11.12	4.5	3.8	na	—	na	—	na	—
AMEV ADVANTAGE-CAP APPRE	AMEV	G	16	12.98	4.5	0.4	na	—	na	—	na	—
AMEV ADVANTAGE-HIGH YLD	AMEV	BPH	20	5.60	4.5	18.1	na	—	na	—	-5.5	97
AMEV CAPITAL FUND, INC.	AMEV	G	135	12.67	4.8	1.9	13.3	25	10.4	25	9.6	40
AMEV FIDUCIARY FUND	AMEV	G	29	20.27	4.5	1.0	na	—	9.8	31	10.1	33
AMEV GROWTH FUND, INC.	AMEV	AG	204	17.47	4.8	1.2	13.5	23	11.3	17	12.9	13

| LATEST 12 MNTHS | | THIS MONTH | | 1990 TO DATE | | CALENDAR YEARS | | | | | | CYCLES | | | | CDA RATING |
| | | | | | | 1989 | | 1988 | | 1987 | | UP MKT | | DOWN MKT | | |
PCNT	RK	PCNT	RK	PCNT	RK%	PCNT	RK	PCNT	RK	PCNT	RK	PCNT	RK	PCNT	RK	
0.8	47	2.8	28	0.8	47	29.4	15	12.5	41	na	—	62.2	21	−11.3	59	21
8.5	10	1.4	55	8.5	10	12.3	59	6.8	81	na	—	22.5	78	3.8	9	17
−15.8	91	4.3	13	−15.8	91	33.3	9	27.3	4	0.2	58	85.8	5	−24.2	92	90
9.7	5	1.5	53	9.7	5	11.7	61	7.1	78	2.8	36	23.2	75	4.0	7	11
−2.0	55	2.5	32	−2.0	55	26.6	20	10.9	53	0.8	51	48.1	37	−11.1	59	36
7.5	14	1.6	51	7.5	14	12.3	59	8.0	72	1.9	43	23.4	75	3.0	14	18
6.3	25	0.5	76	6.3	25	10.8	66	12.2	43	−0.6	63	27.6	58	2.1	26	10
6.2	27	0.5	77	6.2	27	6.2	92	4.6	91	3.7	30	14.4	92	2.9	14	51
−4.6	63	3.5	19	−4.6	63	32.5	10	13.0	37	−16.5	98	75.7	10	−22.9	91	71
−9.2	78	1.8	45	−9.2	78	15.2	48	19.2	16	3.9	28	48.4	37	−17.8	79	71+
−9.8	79	0.7	71	−9.8	79	17.4	43	22.2	10	−16.2	98	21.8	80	−3.1	42	80
−6.1	68	−0.7	95	−6.1	68	34.1	8	15.5	26	−4.0	84	48.7	36	−2.3	41	56+
−17.6	93	3.3	22	−17.6	93	24.8	24	24.4	7	3.4	32	67.5	16	−24.3	92	78+
−7.0	71	0.8	68	−7.0	71	27.6	18	13.3	36	−0.7	64	59.9	23	−15.1	72	64
−1.7	54	4.2	14	−1.7	54	9.1	81	1.9	94	−4.9	86	13.9	92	−11.0	58	81
8.6	9	1.6	49	8.6	9	11.7	61	3.0	93	−4.1	84	16.9	89	3.7	9	33
−5.3	66	3.5	19	−5.3	66	19.6	37	16.7	22	0.1	59	53.1	31	−15.1	72	62
0.8	47	1.8	45	0.8	47	17.7	42	13.4	35	−5.3	87	35.0	48	−3.5	42	15
−8.6	76	2.4	34	−8.6	76	22.2	31	20.9	12	−11.4	96	69.3	14	−22.2	89	79
−17.2	93	6.6	4	−17.2	93	15.7	47	17.3	20	8.6	13	43.4	41	−27.9	95	88+
−6.2	69	1.8	45	−6.2	69	17.5	43	8.8	68	8.3	13	39.1	45	−14.7	71	58+
2.8	42	1.2	60	2.8	42	12.4	58	11.0	52	1.8	44	27.9	57	−0.5	39	22
−5.4	66	2.7	28	−5.4	66	23.5	28	12.6	40	3.8	29	51.3	34	−14.4	69	53+
−12.7	86	−3.7	99	−12.7	86	14.5	50	1.7	94	−11.0	96	24.4	71	−9.0	53	91+
−14.1	88	1.1	63	−14.1	88	−3.6	98	14.0	32	1.7	44	8.7	95	−15.0	71	88+
8.1	11	1.9	42	8.1	11	37.9	5	3.9	92	10.0	10	65.0	17	−5.1	45	20+
−4.1	62	3.3	21	−4.1	62	37.6	5	16.3	24	2.8	36	116.8	1	−29.1	96	75+
−4.0	61	3.2	23	−4.0	61	14.8	49	10.9	54	−12.5	97	42.7	42	−17.4	78	80+
−17.3	93	−1.2	96	−17.3	93	−4.0	98	7.4	75	2.0	42	1.8	97	−12.5	62	90+
9.0	8	1.0	64	9.0	8	10.0	73	5.9	86	na	—	na	—	4.2	6	na
0.9	46	2.7	28	0.9	46	30.7	13	17.6	20	−4.8	86	78.2	8	−13.4	65	23
5.5	33	3.1	24	5.5	33	35.9	7	11.3	50	9.6	11	83.8	6	−13.9	67	33+
6.7	21	7.6	3	6.7	21	63.6	1	17.5	20	−1.5	70	160.2	1	−22.8	90	36
−2.2	55	2.9	26	−2.2	55	13.8	52	16.3	23	0.4	55	36.6	47	−8.1	50	24+
5.5	33	1.6	49	5.5	33	13.0	55	8.2	71	2.7	37	21.3	81	2.4	20	40+
7.9	12	1.3	59	7.9	12	12.5	58	6.5	82	3.7	30	20.9	82	3.6	10	24
−23.9	97	3.1	25	−23.9	97	11.7	61	17.0	21	−6.9	90	31.1	51	−20.6	86	94
−4.7	64	4.0	15	−4.7	64	34.0	8	19.8	14	−1.0	66	62.0	21	−10.9	58	42
−3.0	58	3.8	16	−3.0	58	23.5	28	17.1	21	4.8	23	77.5	9	−20.4	85	72+
−19.9	95	2.8	27	−19.9	95	21.7	32	30.9	2	11.3	9	59.1	24	−14.7	70	79+
−24.9	97	3.9	16	−24.9	97	24.4	25	28.8	4	−3.1	79	85.8	5	−32.1	98	93+
−1.8	54	3.1	23	−1.8	54	25.2	23	16.5	23	0.8	51	60.6	23	−13.5	66	42+
−15.0	89	2.6	30	−15.0	89	−12.9	99	10.2	59	−1.9	73	−13.3	98	−10.1	56	96
−21.0	96	−0.1	91	−21.0	96	29.3	15	33.0	2	−5.8	89	77.8	8	−15.6	73	73+
11.0	3	2.0	40	11.0	3	11.0	65	8.6	69	3.4	32	23.2	75	4.6	4	9
7.4	14	0.3	85	7.4	14	10.3	70	13.3	36	1.3	48	29.6	53	2.9	15	2
7.4	14	0.3	85	7.4	14	10.1	72	14.9	28	−0.2	61	30.5	52	2.4	20	2
6.2	27	0.5	78	6.2	27	10.6	69	13.2	36	−5.5	88	29.6	53	1.2	36	9
7.8	13	0.4	79	7.8	13	9.2	81	11.7	48	−4.0	84	25.8	65	2.7	16	8

(Continued)

LATEST 12 MNTHS		THIS MONTH		1990 TO DATE		CALENDAR YEARS						CYCLES				CDA RATING
						1989		1988		1987		UP MKT		DOWN MKT		
PCNT	RK	PCNT	RK	PCNT	RK%	PCNT	RK	PCNT	RK	PCNT	RK	PCNT	RK	PCNT	RK	
6.9	19	0.4	79	6.9	19	9.8	75	13.0	37	−0.5	63	28.7	55	2.5	19	4
−23.4	97	4.5	12	−23.4	97	28.2	17	29.7	3	−5.3	87	92.0	4	−30.9	97	90+
12.2	2	0.6	74	12.2	2	na	—	na	—	na	—	na	—	5.8	2	na
na	—	0.5	76	na	—	na	—	na	—	na	—	na	—	5.5	2	na
−2.6	57	5.8	6	−2.6	57	6.0	92	0.6	95	18.6	5	55.1	29	−33.4	98	76+
7.7	13	1.0	64	7.7	13	7.7	88	na	—	na	—	na	—	2.7	17	na
1.9	44	0.7	70	1.9	44	8.3	86	7.0	79	na	—	17.8	88	−0.5	39	67
7.3	15	1.2	61	7.3	15	8.4	85	4.8	90	na	—	14.5	92	5.0	3	37
−12.1	84	3.1	24	−12.1	84	19.1	39	10.6	56	−1.8	72	40.8	43	−18.2	81	83+
−10.1	80	1.6	50	−10.1	80	21.6	33	17.5	20	na	—	53.3	31	−16.1	75	76
−10.9	81	2.3	30	−10.9	81	20.4	36	12.5	41	na	—	41.8	43	−17.2	78	80
8.4	10	1.2	60	8.4	10	8.8	84	5.9	86	−0.6	63	18.2	88	2.6	17	57+
−4.1	62	4.3	13	−4.1	62	26.8	20	8.9	67	11.7	9	62.4	20	−21.9	89	65+
−1.6	53	2.9	26	−1.6	53	21.4	33	12.8	39	3.8	29	44.8	40	−10.6	57	28+
−3.4	59	2.1	39	−3.4	59	30.4	14	14.7	29	−0.2	61	71.6	12	−13.9	67	62+
7.1	16	1.8	45	7.1	16	5.2	93	12.9	38	6.3	17	21.5	80	1.9	29	40+
1.9	44	4.7	11	1.9	44	29.0	16	3.6	92	4.0	27	63.8	19	−21.9	89	73+
−2.9	57	3.1	24	−2.9	57	30.9	13	12.0	45	1.1	49	73.0	11	−17.3	78	67+
−4.6	63	2.0	40	−4.6	63	21.7	33	12.6	40	1.6	45	48.0	37	−12.6	63	49+
−5.2	66	2.5	32	−5.2	66	15.5	47	16.1	24	8.8	12	52.7	32	−16.2	75	68+
9.5	6	1.7	46	9.5	6	13.7	53	5.1	89	−1.3	69	22.3	79	4.2	6	14
8.7	9	1.8	44	8.7	9	14.8	49	6.9	80	−1.5	70	24.7	69	4.6	3	5
−1.2	52	1.9	43	−1.2	52	20.6	35	16.7	22	−3.7	83	48.9	36	−8.3	50	31+
−15.6	90	0.0	91	−15.6	90	−11.9	99	13.3	36	2.2	40	−3.5	97	−13.2	65	88+
5.0	36	0.1	89	5.0	36	11.1	65	14.0	31	−6.4	89	29.5	53	1.3	35	43+
−5.9	67	2.6	31	−5.9	67	28.3	17	12.1	45	1.6	46	60.6	23	−16.8	77	71+
6.0	29	0.1	89	6.0	29	10.3	70	7.3	77	−1.6	70	22.5	78	2.0	27	39
6.4	25	0.8	68	6.4	25	9.0	83	9.5	64	−8.1	92	21.3	81	2.1	26	41
5.6	32	0.6	72	5.6	32	10.0	73	8.5	70	−2.5	77	23.1	76	1.9	28	39
5.9	30	0.7	69	5.9	30	10.4	70	9.0	66	−1.2	68	23.2	75	2.1	25	34
5.7	31	0.4	82	5.7	31	9.0	82	8.8	67	−0.1	60	22.7	77	1.9	29	40
−10.5	80	−2.8	98	−10.5	80	na	—	na	—	na	—	na	—	−4.1	43	na
−6.9	71	1.7	48	−6.9	71	24.7	25	8.4	70	3.5	31	33.3	49	−11.1	59	58+
−30.8	99	2.9	26	−30.8	99	6.5	91	1.9	94	−19.7	99	13.5	92	−32.0	98	99+
0.2	48	2.3	35	0.2	48	5.6	93	na	—	na	—	na	—	−7.0	47	na
−17.5	93	0.2	88	−17.5	93	33.5	9	18.5	17	−2.2	75	100.3	3	−27.3	95	97+
−13.4	87	1.2	59	−13.4	87	−12.3	99	9.0	66	5.8	19	−6.4	98	−12.2	62	90+
−1.8	54	4.5	12	−1.8	54	11.7	61	12.1	45	4.7	24	40.3	44	−17.9	80	49+
−1.6	53	2.5	33	−1.6	53	25.1	23	12.8	38	4.6	24	52.2	33	−10.6	57	24+
−3.0	58	1.9	42	−3.0	58	24.3	26	6.0	86	13.3	7	47.5	38	−12.1	61	51+
0.7	47	2.2	37	0.7	47	26.7	20	10.0	61	3.8	29	49.1	36	−5.9	46	30+
na	—	2.0	40	na	—	na	—	na	—	na	—	na	—	na	—	na
na	—	1.0	65	na	—	na	—	na	—	na	—	na	—	na	—	na
na	—	1.3	58	na	—	na	—	na	—	na	—	na	—	na	—	na
−1.1	51	1.9	42	−1.1	51	22.6	30	na	—	na	—	na	—	−8.9	52	na
−14.1	88	4.3	13	−14.1	88	44.7	2	na	—	na	—	na	—	−34.9	99	na
−18.7	94	1.6	49	−18.7	94	−5.3	99	9.5	64	na	—	na	—	−14.2	69	na
−9.5	78	1.6	49	−9.5	78	38.2	5	5.2	89	2.4	38	62.4	20	−18.1	80	70+
−11.1	82	2.0	40	−11.1	82	40.2	4	7.0	79	0.3	56	70.0	13	−20.1	85	77+
−6.3	69	4.0	15	−6.3	69	42.6	3	7.8	73	−0.5	63	86.1	5	−22.7	90	77+

TABLE 6.5 *(Continued)*

FUND	MGT CO	IO	ASSETS MIL$	NAV	MAX LOAD	% DIVD	10 YEARS PCNT	RK	5 YEARS PCNT	RK	3 YEARS PCNT	RK
AMEV SPECIAL STOCK FUND	AMEV	AG	31	21.56	0.0	1.5	12.2	38	10.2	27	13.3	12
AMEV TAX FREE MN PORTF	AMEV	MB	25	9.68	4.5	6.2	na	—	na	—	8.0	67
AMEV TAX FREE NATL PORTF	AMEV	MB	40	9.82	4.5	6.5	na	—	na	—	8.0	67
AMEV US GOV SECURITIES	AMEV	BPG	171	9.76	4.5	8.9	12.3	37	9.2	40	10.0	33
ANALYTIC OPTIONED EQUITY	ANALYT	GI	101	11.92	0.0	3.8	10.8	62	9.7	31	11.4	20
API TRUST	API	AG	22	9.38	0.0	0.0	na	—	5.8	83	8.3	63
ARMSTRONG ASSOCIATES	PORTFO	G	9	6.26	0.0	3.6	na	—	7.4	71	7.2	75
ASSOCIATED PLANNERS STK	APS	G	17	16.25	4.8	0.7	na	—	14.6	6	14.6	7
AXE-HOUGHTON FUND B	EW-AXE	B	156	8.99	5.8	6.0	12.7	32	11.0	20	12.1	16
AXE-HOUGHTON GROWTH FUND	EW-AXE	AG	64	6.72	5.8	0.7	9.0	80	7.5	70	11.3	21
AXE-HOUGHTON INCOME	EW-AXE	BPC	63	4.85	4.8	7.6	12.3	36	8.0	61	7.6	71

Annualized ROR thru 12/31/90

Source: CDA Investment Technologies, Inc. Reprinted by permission.

If that is the case, what should you be looking for in reaching conclusions regarding the People question? What are the good signs? What are the bad signs? Let's put together a checklist for evaluating "People."

Management Systems

There are two main management systems in the fund industry—committee and star—and each in turn provides numerous variations on a theme.

Committee:

This system is generally exemplified by an organization with a strong central investment policy committee. This committee will be comprised of the main investment professionals within the organization who are receiving analytical and research inputs concerning the economy, global and domestic politics, and the monetary situation, as well as specific equity and debt market developments.

(Continued)

LATEST 12 MNTHS		THIS MONTH		1990 TO DATE		CALENDAR YEARS						CYCLES				CDA RATING
						1989		1988		1987		UP MKT		DOWN MKT		
PCNT	RK	PCNT	RK	PCNT	RK%	PCNT	RK	PCNT	RK	PCNT	RK	PCNT	RK	PCNT	RK	
−4.3	62	4.4	12	−4.3	62	40.9	4	7.8	73	−6.8	90	83.3	6	−22.6	90	74+
6.2	26	0.3	83	6.2	26	8.2	86	9.6	63	−0.6	63	21.5	81	2.4	21	38
5.3	34	0.3	86	5.3	34	8.9	83	10.0	61	1.2	48	22.9	76	1.4	34	44
10.4	3	1.5	53	10.4	3	12.4	58	7.3	77	3.7	30	23.8	73	4.8	3	36+
1.5	45	2.3	36	1.5	45	17.8	42	15.6	26	4.2	26	46.9	38	−7.9	50	31+
−12.7	86	12.5	1	−12.7	86	15.6	47	26.0	5	−7.7	91	57.6	26	−30.9	97	92
−6.7	71	2.0	40	−6.7	71	14.1	51	15.7	26	4.1	26	47.5	38	−13.4	65	67+
2.2	43	2.0	40	2.2	43	37.8	5	6.9	79	13.2	7	60.6	13	−10.5	57	14
7.2	16	1.8	43	7.2	16	20.6	35	8.9	66	−4.0	84	39.9	44	−0.1	39	15+
6.4	25	5.5	7	6.4	25	29.8	14	−0.2	95	−6.2	89	52.7	32	−14.4	69	58+
4.2	39	1.3	59	4.2	39	10.2	71	8.7	68	1.8	44	21.3	81	0.9	37	53+

These inputs are synthesized down into a policy governing overall portfolio direction, and more specifically a positive, neutral, or negative position on stocks and bonds. The economy is expanding, therefore . . . The Federal Reserve is tightening money supply, therefore . . . Interest rates are declining, which will benefit the following industries. . . And so forth.

In a strict committee system, the portfolio manager of a specific fund within that group becomes no more than a glorified order filler. The manager has little or no control over the composition of his portfolio. If it is an equity fund, for instance, cash percentage, industry concentrations, and specific issues are fairly well dictated by the committee. The manager buys only those stocks that the committee has cleared for the approved list, period.

In a quasi-committee system, the portfolio manager has much more input into the complexion of the fund's portfolio. The committee might set down general guidelines, very broad parameters, but the final say rests with the manager. For instance, the committee might say cash can never go below 5 percent or above 25 percent; where the total is at any given point in time within that range is up to the manager. The committee might say no industry concentrations above 20 percent; which industries are built up at any time is up to the manager. Quite a different set of circumstances from the prior form.

Star:

The star system represents the bulk of the mutual fund industry. However much industry officials may deny it, the fact is the results of most funds can be ascribed to the talents of a single individual. With the growing notoriety of the fund industry within the investment world, these stars have attained the status of icons.

Peter Lynch (whose announced retirement in mid-1990 became a media event unto itself), John Neff, John Templeton, Mario Gabelli, Dick Strong, Bob Stowers, and others are the magi of mutual funds.

In certain cases, the star system is truly a one-person show. The people in it are innovators, loners, solitary thinkers. They chafe at the slightest hint of bureaucracy. In other situations, while there might be a strong lead personality functioning as the star, he or she makes use of a very strong support system—a structure that nurtures the capabilities of the star.

The bottom line is that both the committee approach and the star system can work in all their various forms. What you, the investor, must determine is what suits your tastes, what matches your psyche. Will you lose sleep if your money is managed by a strong-willed iconoclast, or is your temperament better suited to a fund managed by a committee? Can you identify with the idiosyncracies displayed by trendsetters, or are you more at ease with the stability of a group approach? These are the judgments you must make.

As an overview, let's look at the pros and cons of each avenue:

Committee	*Star*

Pros

Manager turnover not so critical	Manager's reputation is on the line every day
Built-in support	Ego satisfaction
	Investing is intuitive; intuition flourishes in star system

Cons

"A camel is a horse built by a committee"	Support system critical
	Manager turnover can prove terminal
	New star equals brand new fund
	Constant monitoring critical

These last few points regarding the negatives of the star system deserve amplification. When a star leaves a fund, your analysis must go back to square one. Past performance becomes meaningless; all assessments were made on assumptions no longer valid. Monitoring is critical, because if there is a manager change, you must assess the qualifications of the successor as soon as possible. Some lag time does exist—the new manager would be foolhardy to make wholesale liquidations in his or her predecessor's portfolio. (The reverse also holds true. If you follow a star to a new fund, it will take some time before he or she can reshape the portfolio to their tastes.)

Longevity of Personnel

In a word, *stay away from funds with a revolving door*. Management stability or consistency is critical to the success of funds. If the senior management of the fund group cannot induce capable managers to stay, you as an investor must constantly be concerned over their ability to continue to attract capable managers.

There is another element at work here: what if the manager responsible for the historically consistent track record is no longer there? Buying a fund because it has a good consistent track record, even though the individual responsible for that record has already left, is as productive as closing the barn door after the cow is out.

How do you know if the fund group you are considering has a good record in terms of retaining managers? Simple enough—ask! Call up the group or your broker and ask them how long the manager currently at the helm of the fund you are considering for purchase has been there. How long was his or her predecessor there? If you don't have the time for such calls, don't despair. Many financial publications that regularly cover the fund world will now show the name of the current portfolio manager of featured funds and how long they have filled that role.

Clearly, this is a much more critical issue in funds run on the star system than in those run by committee. If the star is calling all the shots and the star leaves, that is the definition of critical. But even in management by committee, personnel turnover takes on importance. Constant turnover of the individuals who together constitute the investment policy committee will likewise lead to a lack of consistency. Many a person from a fund led by committee has bragged to me about how many years each member of this committee had in the industry and with their firm.

The Work Environment

The buzzword for this is "corporate culture," and it is an essential part of a group's ability to retain managers. It brings to mind a discussion I had some years ago with a member of senior management of a database management firm. I was curious how a firm such as his retained those oddball rogues known as computer whizzes. Money was obviously not uppermost in their minds.

His answer was quite succinct. I was absolutely right—money counted for very little to these geniuses. What counted was environment—having coworkers of a similar ilk, ready access to whatever hardware or software they deemed necessary to their work, an open office layout, no need to toe the line vis-à-vis maintaining a corporate look, and so on.

The same is true for mutual funds. An environment conducive to creative thinking is no less critical in a fund management firm than it is in a computer hardware/software outfit. A think-tank, professional atmosphere with cultivation and cross-fertilization of ideas and ready access to research resources will provide a fund with a competitive edge. As we shall see when we discuss the third "P"—Process—discipline is a key ingredient in tortoise funds. However, investment discipline (a critical ingredient) should not be mistaken for corporate discipline, the tie-and-jacket syndrome.

Coming as I do from the straight-laced corporate environment of midtown Manhattan, I recall vividly how I was momentarily taken aback when first visiting the offices of a successful Rocky Mountain–based fund group. Nowhere, I repeat, nowhere was there a jacket to be seen. Those with sweaters and ties probably considered themselves dressed up. Chinos and loafers appeared to be the dress code. But the more I spoke to the key players, the more I appreciated how much high-quality work was being generated by this group.

Another example of good working conditions can be seen in the offices of a leading Boston-based fund group. All the key portfolio managers have offices in close proximity to one another and share access to the "war room"—a

large oval room in the center of the floor where current
and historical charts and data regarding every aspect of the
investment process overwhelm the space. Quite frequently
while I was visiting with one of the managers, an associate
would knock on the door, come in and begin a skull session on an idea he was germinating.

*A good work environment leads to good investment re-
turns.* I grant you analysis of the work environment is
beyond the realm of the typical investor. Nevertheless,
some attempt (stories regarding same in financial magazines, reviews in publications devoted to the fund industry,
a visit to a local fund group) should be made. It's not that
you can't properly assess whether a fund belongs in your
portfolio without making a judgment regarding its work
environment. Rather, it's simply another piece of the
puzzle.

Support System

Regardless of whether a fund is run on the star or committee system, the research and analysis resources within the
firm will determine whether that fund consistently deliv-
ers above-average returns.

Rule: *Mutual funds that rely on Wall Street research as
their primary source of ideas are predoomed to mediocrity.*

With all due respects to our brethren in the brokerage
community, a fund cannot develop an "edge" on its competitors by relying on information that is being dissemi-
nated to hundreds of institutions simultaneously. To
succeed, a fund must be able to generate investment ideas
internally. Some support might come from external
sources, but the firm must be equipped with a sufficient
number of research people and analysts to allow the star
or committee to build a portfolio based on their own ideas.

The larger the fund group and the broader the investment approach it utilizes, the more resources it will re-

quire. One large West Coast fund complex employs over 35 specialists, including a convertible bond analyst, a researcher for technology stocks, government bonds, autos, high-yield bonds, etc. Given the speed with which markets move today, with the maze of events constantly unfolding in each of these subsets of the stock and bond markets, each area requires full-time coverage. If a fund group expects to "cover the waterfront," some combination of research people and analysts numbering in the 20s, 30s, or perhaps in the 40s, employed by the firm or whose expertise is readily accessible from outside sources, is required.

On the other hand, a small fund group, or especially a stand-alone fund, can get by very ably with a veritable handful of research people. In fact, in many such situations—most of which are run on the star system—the portfolio managers themselves will also serve as analysts. One of the most successful Midwest small fund groups does quite well with fewer than five in the support group; in this case, the stars do wear two hats: portfolio managers and analysts.

Three forms of support systems can be identified in the fund world: (1) Totally internal. All research and analysis performed by staff. No reliance at all on brokerage house–generated ideas. (2) Primarily internal. The bulk of themes developed by staff. Internally generated ideas substantiated by external sources. Some ideas provided by third-party research. (3) Primarily external. Ideas externally sourced, developed internally.

The first is the least common. It may be preferable to generate ideas by your own analysts, but sometimes it helps to have two sets of ears. The second is the most common. As an example, the Midwest group referred to above generates most of its ideas by itself, but looks to small, regional brokerage firms to come up with some special situations. When I asked how much weight they gave to Wall Street research, the answer was rather direct—

"None!" The third form—primarily external—is, as we said earlier, a formula for failure. You cannot excel at portfolio management without a serious commitment to research and analysis.

How do you learn the depth of the support system in the fund you are considering? Same answer as before—ask! How many portfolio managers do you have? Do they also perform research? How many people in your organization are involved in research (and their average years of experience)? Are most ideas internally generated? What role does brokerage-house research, Wall Street or regional, play in your decision-making process? Most organizations now have shareholder-servicing agents qualified to answer such questions. If not, inquire whether you may submit your questions in writing.

Let us recap. Good managers make good funds. Most tortoise funds are headed by stars; committee-dominated tortoise funds are the exception to the rule. Most tortoise fund managers have been at the helm for a considerable period of time. A favorable work environment is conducive to good investment results. Successful funds have sufficient research and analysis resources to internally develop most of their investment themes.

PROCESS

Security analysis is a multifaceted activity. Typically, analysts identify stocks of companies with good track records, and then meet with the senior management of these companies to learn their operating philosophies and strategy. In a similar fashion, in mutual fund analysis we first find those funds with good, consistent track records (*Performance*). We then learn more about the qualifications of those at the helm (*People*). Now we must define the fund's operating philosophy/strategy (*Process*).

Process defines the specific style of investing employed

by the fund's portfolio manager to achieve its stated investment objective. *Process is not to be confused with objective.* The process/style is the means to the desired end (objective).

This is the trap into which many an investor falls. "Mr. Jones, what style of investing does your fund use?" To which Jones replies, "Aggressive growth." Wrong! That is its objective, its goal. How does it hope to get there? By investing in emerging growth stocks, cyclicals, turnaround situations, small-cap stocks, high-tech stocks? What techniques does the fund manager employ? Does he or she use earnings screens, dividend screens, stocks trading at a fraction or multiple of market ratios?

Simply put, all roads may lead to Rome, but they are not all the same. This is Process—defining the particular characteristics of each road. An aggressive growth fund is not an aggressive growth fund is not an aggressive growth fund. A bond fund is not a bond fund is not a bond fund. (Sorry, Gertrude!)

Why is discerning each fund's process so critical? For a number of reasons. First, by owning a variety of funds that in turn utilize a variety of investment styles, you will be able to better *smooth out market cycles.* Put another way, you will flatten the roller coaster ride. Not all styles work in every market environment. There will be times when value stocks are outperforming growth stocks and other times when the reverse is true. If you have clearly defined the process used by each candidate and purchased a variety of styles, some portion of your portfolio will always be working for you (more about this later).

Second, owning a variety of styles *protects against overlap.* The more differentiated the process in your fund lineup, the less likely the funds are to be buying and selling off the same list of stocks or bonds. A simple example: if Manager A specializes in high-cap stocks with consistent dividend increases and Manager B specializes in small-cap stocks with earnings growth per year double that of the average stock, how likely is it that they will ever be buying or selling the same stocks? This is how you achieve true numerical diversification.

Third, clearly defining each fund's area of expertise leads to true *manager diversification.* As you will recall, when we defined the various facets of investment risk, one of them was manager risk. We saw that there was a high probability that at some point each manager is going to make a mistake. Good managers goof less frequently than poor managers, but all the same they err. The way around this state of affairs is to own multiple managers. Without checking for process, simply owning more than one fund is preferable to owning only one (even if they all employ the same process). But the way to optimize the risk-averse characteristics of a multi-manager portfolio is to undertake the necessary research and insure that it's also a multi-style portfolio.

How do you define a manager's process/style? There are a number of tools available. The first step is to define the particular "playing field" on which they seem to be most comfortable.

PLAYING FIELD

Stocks	*Bonds*
High cap	Treasuries
Low cap	Agencies
High tech	Corporates
Low tech	Long term
Industry leaders	Intermediate term
Emerging companies	Short term
Specific industries	Convertibles

Some managers are most comfortable playing on only one field, others use a combination, while yet others will play the field, finding opportunities wherever they may be.

Next, you must define what specific approaches or biases

the manager utilizes in the selection of individual stocks and bonds.

APPROACHES/BIASES

Stocks	*Bonds*
Bottom-up vs. top-down	Bottom-up vs. top-down
Screens: earnings, dividends, balance sheet	Equity valuation first
Value vs. growth	Interest rate anticipation or not
Undervalued (vs. market, vs. itself)	Fixed maturity vs. floating maturity
Fundamental vs. modern portfolio theory	Fixed grade vs. mixed grades

These constitute the epitome of Process—the clear definition of the stocks or bonds with which the manager feels most comfortable, and the specific tools, approaches, biases the manager utilizes in the selection process—in other words, the discipline employed in creating the fund's portfolio. If you cannot define that discipline, stay away! Even if a fund has had a consistent track record and a stable management team, they mean nothing if they were not the result of a well-defined investment process. Shooting from the hip might work for a while, but it is only a matter of time before it blows up in your face. *An undisciplined manager is a time bomb waiting to go off.*

Fortunately, there are a number of ways to double-check your homework, to make sure you have properly defined a fund's process.

Back Check

This is a test for consistency. The fund manager may tell you he employs a certain investment style, and a check of the current annual or semi-annual report might seem to bear it out. But does this also hold true if you check that fund's portfolio six months, one year, or two years earlier? I am not talking about turnover. The specific stocks or bonds in the portfolio might change, but are the new names cut from the same cloth? If the manager tells you he or she is most comfortable with high-cap stocks, and the semiannual report of a year ago shows a portfolio heavily concentrated in small-cap stocks, then something has been lost between the lip and the cup. (Or worse yet, you've been duped!)

Articulation

I do not expect every fund manager to be a great communicator, but many years of personal experience have shown me that if fund managers cannot articulate their investment process, that is a chink in their discipline. They must be able to set out for you quite clearly the methodology they employ on a day-to-day basis. Conveying an investment style does not take superior communication skills. Quite the opposite—often a skillfully worded investment policy statement can be a smoke screen to cover an ill-begotten process. A great deal of sizzle does not compensate for little steak.

How important is articulation? I recall an interview some time ago with the new portfolio manager of a fund with a most admirable long-term track record. I asked him whether he intended to run the fund as his predecessor had. His response was, "For the most part." This wasn't the worst of it; that came next. "How will you select the stocks which you purchase for the fund?" "Well, I have a lot of friends around the Street, and they're always calling me with ideas." My associate who had accompanied me on this interview actually turned pale at that moment.

This incident, of course, corroborates two points I have been trying to convey. One, the importance of people in the

---

Where Not to Go for Information

One would think that the "Investment Objective" or similarly titled section of a fund's prospectus would be the perfect place for fund management to articulate its investment process/style. Unfortunately, such is not the case. A prospectus is a legal document which binds the fund. As with all legal documents, it is worded in generalities, rather than specifics. There are exceptions, of course, but for the most part a fund's prospectus will not articulate anything more than its objective, and then only in the broadest of terms. "The Fund seeks capital appreciation, with current income being a secondary consideration." Thanks a lot!

---

mutual fund equation, and why one must be so vigilant regarding manager turnover. Two, the role articulation plays in verifying the existence or lack of a process.

Top Ten Holdings

In a typical fund, the ten largest positions will generally account for 25–50 percent of the assets. If you know a fund's ten largest holdings, you have a pretty good fix on how it is going to perform. Plus, you have a good read of its process.

If you believe you have identified some funds that have made it through the performance and people screens, and have now been qualified by representing a variety of processes, run the following acid test: compare their ten largest holdings against one another. For instance, if you believe you have identified five aggressive growth funds with distinct and unique styles, write up a master list of their ten largest holdings. The optimum would be that you come up with fifty stocks (five times ten per fund). More realistically, you will find some overlap.

There are no hard and fast rules, but again from personal experience I believe overlap of more than 25 percent (12–13 names appearing more than once) would indicate that you have not done a good job of defining process. The lines of demarcation should not be that fuzzy. What you believe are five investment styles may in reality be no more than two or three.

I recently ran this test on groups of twelve aggressive growth funds, twelve conservative growth funds and ten growth and income funds. Since I was looking at their ten largest holdings, the optimum number for both the aggressive growth and conservative growth pools was 120. In reality, overlap in both cases was less than 20 percent. In the growth and income group, the overlap was slightly greater than 20 percent, but we expected this since the pool of stocks that might appear in a growth and income portfolio is considerably smaller than that of conservative or aggressive growth stocks.

To further corroborate that we had optimized numerical *and* style diversification we actually ran a further litmus test. We created a "master portfolio" from each group of top ten holdings, with each position being given a pro rata weighting. For instance, if the master portfolio was made up of ten different funds and XYZ Corp. represented 2.5 percent of one component fund and did not appear in any other portfolio, it would represent 0.25 percent of the master.

In each pool—aggressive growth, conservative growth, growth and income—only one stock represented more than 1.0 percent of the master portfolio, with the average weighting being far below 0.3 percent! That is the essence of numerical and style diversification.

How does one go about getting the necessary information to make an informed judgment about process? There are a number of ways:

1. The fund's prospectus. As we said earlier, this unfortunately is an unlikely source. However, you may luck out and find your fund is the exception to the rule.

2. The fund's annual and semi-annual reports. Likely to be much more descriptive. If the detail is not in the letter to shareholders, check "largest positions," "purchases and sales," or the full portfolio itself for clues.

3. Publications. Mutual fund managers are now being interviewed in publications such as *Barron's,* the *Wall Street Journal, Forbes, Business Week, Financial World, Mutual Fund Values,* and *Wiesenberger.* If the interview is probing enough, you should have a good sense of the manager's investment style.

4. Ask. Our standard fallback position. Call or write the fund in which you are interested and ask them the key questions: any particular area of specialization, favorite playing field, techniques, approaches, biases, etc.

SUMMARY

Tortoise funds are few and far between. Correct implementation of the "Three P's" will screen out over 95 percent of all funds. Why go to all the trouble? Why not simply follow the advice of some advisory letters, buy funds featured in business magazines, select funds randomly or by tips?

The answer: investing only in tortoise funds will (1) reduce the probability of subsequent heartaches (tortoises don't put you on the roller coaster); and (2) reduce turnover (tortoises are much more consistent over the long term than hares).

You *must* do the homework. Consistent, "boring" tor-

Odds and Ends

There are a number of miscellaneous questions I am often asked about fund selection that should be given some attention:

Q: Should I focus solely on no-load funds?

A: No, in applying the selection criteria enumerated above you will likely identify a cross section of both load and no-load tortoise funds. Since your intention is to own a number of them and hold them for a considerable period of time (remember they are tortoises), if you occasionally incur a 4–5–6–8 percent load, it will not detrimentally affect you. If you purchase ten funds, half of which are no-load and half of which have an average load of 5 percent, then the average load for the entire portfolio is 2½ percent, which is quite reasonable. Plus, this is a round-trip expense since in mutual funds you only pay once—on the way in or the way out.

Q: Is there any difference between front-load and back-load funds?

A: Quite a bit! Front-load funds, the traditional type, charge you a commission at the time of purchase, and the salesman is paid from this load. Back-load funds, on the other hand, or deferred-sales-charge funds as they are also called, also pay the salesman up front even though you only pay the sales charge at the time of liquidation some months or years later. How is this possible? Built into such funds' cost structures is a distribution fee (also called a 12b1 fee) of as much as 1–1½ percent annually, which is used to finance the commission paid to the salesman up front. Assume the fund you are considering for purchase has a 12b1 fee of 1¼ percent annually. If you hold that fund for eight to ten years (a reasonable expectation for a tortoise fund), then indirectly you paid a load of 10–12½ percent. That is outrageous! In a word: *Don't buy back-load funds!*

Q: Why not buy last year's underperformers? Will they not bounce back?

A: There is an entire fund investment approach being founded on this theory. There are a couple of problems with it, however. First, we are trying to create stability in our portfolio. Buying underperformers in the hopes they become overperformers will heighten *volatility,* not *stability.* Second, there are no guarantees. An underperformer in year one might overperform in year two, but then again it might not. If it doesn't, you've likely sunk your money into a chronic underperformer.

Q: Aren't closed-end funds basically the same as open-ended funds?

A: No, they are worlds apart—mostly in terms of liquidity. As we noted earlier, an open-ended fund allows you to get in and out of the market when you want. A closed-end fund, by comparison, trades like listed stocks. You need to find a seller when you want to buy, and you must find a buyer when it comes time to sell. What if there are none around? Second, with open-ended funds you trade at net asset value. Closed-end funds often trade at premiums or more often at discounts to net asset value. This is a variable with which you would have to deal. Theoretically, the market may not have moved from the time you bought a closed-end fund until you sold it, but if its discount widened in the interim, you suffer a loss.

Q: How about selecting funds on the basis of expense ratios, turnover rates, asset size, etc.?

A: Boondoggles all! I have seen "scholarly" presentations about each and every one of these, plus many more that are frankly even more nonsensical. Let us put a few of these to rest. Expense ratios: a fund's net asset value is just that—*net* of expenses. If Fund A has an expense ratio of 1%, but has consistently returned an average of 15% per annum, and Fund B has an expense ratio of 0.5%, and an erratic average annual return of 10%, would anyone in their right mind prefer Fund B? Turnover rates: Fund A turns over its portfolio 200% per year and averages 14% return. Fund B turns its portfolio over only 50% per year and returns 10% per year. Do I have any takers for Fund B? Repeat: there are only three criteria for fund selection; the Three P's—Performance (which is net of expenses, turnover, etc.), People, and Process. Everything else is extraneous. Period.

toise funds rarely make it into the headlines. When the markets are rising, which funds are featured? Those that are up 40 percent while the market has risen 20 percent (hares). Who is featured when the market is plummeting? Funds that are down more than the market (hares). Tortoises simply don't have the necessary pizazz to make it to the limelight, but please remember you're not investing for excitement.

Here, then, is the checklist for your homework:

1. Performance

a. Search for consistency.
b. Stay away from cumulative performance.
c. Stay away from "novas."
d. Beware of the Fund du Jour.
e. Thou shalt not buy sector funds!
f. A simple test: above-average performers for three consecutive years.

2. People

a. People run funds, not vice versa.
b. Define the fund's management system: star or committee.

c. How well does the fund retain personnel?
d. Is there a productive work environment?
e. Identify the depth of the manager's research and analysis support system.

3. Process

a. Process equals style.
b. A fund's investment objective is its "end"; the process is the means towards that end.
c. An aggressive growth fund is not an aggressive growth fund is not an aggressive growth fund.
d. Define the fund's area of expertise, its "playing field."
e. Define the manager's selection techniques.
f. Thou shalt have discipline.

Conclusion: Consistent performance is the result of consistent management applying consistent, disciplined investment approaches.

7

THE SEARCH FOR
THE BULLETPROOF
PORTFOLIO

THERE ARE two basic approaches to portfolio construction. The first, unfortunately, is the route most often taken by investors. Namely, haphazard. Through a random series of purchases, a portfolio is almost inadvertently created. The focus is on the individual securities rather than on the whole. The sum of the parts in this case is less than the whole.

I recall meeting with a prospective client some years ago, a highly regarded attorney. He set forth in front of me his "portfolio," using the term lightly. Mishmash is much more descriptive. What I was looking at was a compendium of over 200 different stocks for which there seemed to be no rhyme or reason. What was the unifying thread, I inquired of the prospect. His answer nearly floored me— he had a number of brokers who called him periodically with tips. Whatever they touted, he bought!

That's one way to build a portfolio. The other is the more reasoned approach—looking at your investments as a cohesive whole. Each piece is an integral part of the overall game plan, the portfolio. We know what these pieces are— tortoise funds. Now we have to define how we can most effectively use them in a portfolio context—a portfolio that will allow us to win by not losing—the bulletproof portfolio.

Earlier, we looked at some of the guiding principles behind the concept of winning by not losing. Let's review them now as we place them in portfolio context:

1. Screw Your Head on Backwards

The purposes of our portfolio will be to minimize losses, not maximize gains. The risk of losses has shown us clearly that losses have a much greater impact on the ultimate success or failure of our portfolio than do gains. Stop worrying how your portfolio performs in up markets!

2. Our Portfolio Must Be Able to Withstand Downdrafts and Ongoing Turbulence

By owning (indirectly) thousands of issues, not tens of issues, we will mute event shock. Adverse events, whether they affect individual issues (lower than expected earnings, failed mergers, downgrades, etc.), or entire industry groups (changes in commodity prices, interest rates, regulations, etc.), are a constant way of life in today's investment world.

There's no getting away from them. The only way to minimize their effect is to diffuse it over a widely diversified portfolio.

So it is with market cycles. Remember, *after every hill is a valley*. Fortunately, different types of securities and different investment styles reach their valleys at different times. Therefore, a portfolio with proper asset-class diversification and proper manager diversification will never find itself too deep in the valley.

3. The Bulletproof Portfolio Is an Investment Insurance Policy

We are willing to pay the premiums in the up markets, the premiums being below-average performance resulting from super-diversification. Why? Because we will collect in the down markets. This is one way to help you appreciate what it means to screw your head on backwards. Think about this analogy. Do you feel bad when you pay the premiums on your life insurance policies? Does it bother you that one of your associates had more disposable income because he or she saved the expense of premiums?

Obviously not. Neither should it bother you when your fellow investors outperform you in bull markets. Not if you realize that such underperformance (premium) will be more than compensated for in the next bear market.

4. The Bulletproof Portfolio Smooths Out the Ride

As I said at the very beginning of the book, the markets today are nothing short of roller coasters. They are still capable over the long term of delivering the types of returns that historically have attracted people to stocks and bonds, but the ride has scared away the faint of heart. What we are attempting to achieve is a smoother ride (Figure 7.1)

Remember, we do not expect miracles. When the tide heads out, when markets go down, so will your portfolio. But it will be down considerably less. When the tide comes back in, when the market is rising, so will your portfolio, but again, considerably less. In a word, no bragging rights

FIGURE 7.1

The Smoother Ride

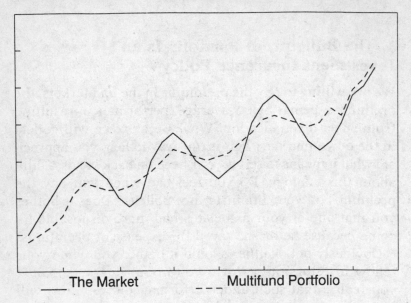

___ The Market   _ _ _ Multifund Portfolio

at the country club. Bulletproof portfolios simply don't excel in up markets. But who cares? Look at the two performance tracks in Figure 7.1. Which do you prefer your portfolio to follow? The "boring" dotted line or the "exciting" solid line? I vote for the "boring" performance. As one of my poetic friends put it, when you follow the principles of winning by not losing, your performance will "chop off the hills and fill in the valleys."

5. Stop Thinking of Performance in Absolute Terms

Let us say your portfolio consists of two investments: U.S. Treasury Bills and raw land. You check at the end of the year and find that each has given you a 10 percent return. Would you say that both performed equally well? Clearly not! On an absolute basis, yes. But on a risk-adjusted basis, no.

There is a cost to investing—peace of mind, volatility— and the higher the cost (risk), the higher your return should be. A high-risk investment that yields the same returns as a low-risk investment is a failure. Period!

In security analysis, we talk about ROI, or Return on Investment. I am now extending that concept to Return on Risk. Absolute performance is at best a blurry sign of how your portfolio is doing; risk-adjusted performance is where it's at.

What we are seeking from our portfolio, therefore, is:

1. Reasonable absolute performance. Remember, the price for peace of mind is that your portfolio will not excel in rising markets. It will excel in declining markets, but most people unfortunately have their heads screwed on straight. They aren't interested if their portfolio declined only 15 percent in the face of a 30 percent retreat by the overall market.

2. We want to achieve *above-average risk-adjusted returns.* If the risk levels in our portfolio have plunged much more precipitously than absolute returns, then our risk-adjusted returns have risen. How do you measure risk? There arc a number of technical means available (the Sharpe Index et al.), but even the layman can measure it subjectively. Do you dread picking up the newspaper the morning after a market calamity to check prices? If not, you've reduced risks. Do you realize that you've stopped reacting negatively to doom and gloom headlines about individual companies because your portfolio now consists solely of tortoise funds? If so, you've reduced risks. If the month-to-month variation in your portfolio's value is never more than a couple of percentage points, you've reduced risks.

3. In the final analysis what you want is *reasonable gains*

(not wealth) with limited risk. It's not risk-free, but it's awful close.

6. "The Sleep-Well-at-Night Portfolio"

One of my marketing people has been begging me for years to allow him to use this phrase in our sales literature, so I include it here out of deference to him. All joking aside, this is the essence of what we are attempting to accomplish. When people cashed in their tax-free bonds in the spring of 1987 or their stock portfolios after the October 1987 crash, why did they do it? They couldn't sleep at night worrying about their investments. If you can't take the heat, get out of the kitchen.

Some years ago, my wife Jane accompanied me on a press interview. The reporter asked her what she considered most noteworthy about me as an investor. Her answer, which appeared in his column, was that in all the years she has known me, I had never lost a night's sleep worrying about a client's portfolio.

That's what it's all about. Peace of mind. Sleeping well. The sense of security normally afforded only by short-term cash equivalents. As some would say, having your cake and eating it too. The types of returns stocks and bonds can provide over the long term coupled with savings vehicles—like lack of volatility. The best of both worlds.

One final vignette on this subject: after the crash of Monday, 19 October 1987, the *New York Times* in its daily editions for some time afterwards ran a special section on how the investment community was reacting to the crash. Towards the end of the first postcrash week, one of these special items concerned a prestigious New York City–based investment management firm whose principals had stayed in the office for three consecutive days. Food and changes of clothing were sent in, etc., etc. Planning session piled on top of crisis session piled on top of policy meeting. (Do you see the grist here for another Oliver Stone "Wall Street" movie?)

My staff and I roared with laughter over this account. We had gone home on time every single evening that week. No panic, no crisis. Some losses, but nothing insurmountable (even clients who had joined us at the very peak a little over a month earlier were back in the black by 1988's second quarter). As I said earlier, if you want excitement, go to Las Vegas. If you want safe, steady returns, read on.

8

BUILDING BULLETPROOF PORTFOLIOS

UNTIL NOW we have been talking about the "why" of winning by not losing. Now we will look at the "how." This is the practical side of the story—how to build a portfolio that will minimize losses in a down market and allow reasonable gains in an up market. And remember, our portfolio will not be an accumulation of randomly selected securities. Rather it will be a cohesive whole, with each piece fulfilling a specific role.

Go back to the sports analogy. As portfolio designers, we play the role of the football coach. We set up the game plan (investment objective), employing the combined talents of our players (tortoise funds) in defined interrelationships between receivers, linemen and backfield (aggressive growth funds, conservative growth funds, etc.) to achieve victory.

One additional thought: just as a game plan is implemented all at once, so should an investment policy. The coach doesn't send only a few players out on the field; the entire team goes on. So in investing. Deploy all your assets at once! The reference, of course, is to dollar-cost averaging, where your capital is deployed over a period of time. That might be fine when putting all your money into one or a limited number of investments; you can't judge when the optimum time is to purchase that security, so instead you buy it piecemeal over a period of time.

We, by comparison, are focused solely on *portfolio* investing. There is *no* way of knowing which component of the portfolio should be purchased when, unless one is in possession of a crystal ball. Do you buy the growth and income funds now and the bond funds later? Or do you purchase small amounts of each at the same time? Do you put off purchasing your aggressive growth funds until stock market conditions improve?

You can drive yourself crazy worrying about such things, or on the other hand sleep easy with the knowledge that all your investments are tortoise funds. They will not cause you horrible losses, even if you happen to be investing at the very onset of a market decline. In addition to which you will have further reduced risk by allocating your assets over different types of funds, further reducing the possibility of insurmountable losses.

The bottom line: *Don't dollar-cost average, and don't put off beginning until market tone is better* (unless you have a crystal ball).

A case in point: when our investment policy committee met in late 1986, our assessment was that the market (the Dow Jones Industrial Average then at about 1900) was slightly overvalued. By historical fundamental valuations, we believed 1700 was a more reasonable level. What to do with new accounts accepted at that point? Wait until the market declined to where we thought it belonged, or alternatively feed the investments in gradually (a.k.a. dollar-cost averaging)? In reality, we chose neither of these paths. We created multifund portfolios according to the guidelines I will describe, enjoyed the gains from the additional

800 points that the average rose betwecn January and August, gave back some of those gains during the ensuing decline (at its low on 19 October our December forecast came to pass—the market *did* decline to 1700), and finished the year comfortably in the black.

Moral: *There is no better time to invest than now.* If you are a true long-term investor and if you accept the principles of winning by not losing, then even if subsequent events prove you started investing at a market high, in the long term you will still come out far ahead. *Don't try to time the market!* But more on that later.

So how does one build a bulletproof portfolio? It's a three-step process: objective setting, asset/sector allocation, and mutual fund selection.

OBJECTIVE SETTING

To properly set your objective you must focus on a number of factors.

Purpose

Simply, why are you investing? To create a nest egg for retirement? To provide for children's educational expenses? To supplement other sources of income out of which you will pay living expenses? To build up your estate? There are myriad reasons why people invest, and you should have a clear understanding of your personal situation before you begin.

Time Frame

This event for which you are planning, how much longer until it occurs? A year, three years, five years, longer? It is important to set the time frame, because, to repeat, investing is a *long-term* process. The problem is to define "long term." Some would say long term is five years, others three years. My own opinion: If you don't have at least three years until you will begin tapping into your portfolio's principal, don't invest in the first place! Remember, we are not attempting to time the market; there are no guarantees as to which direction the markets will head once you begin investing. What if you happen to come in at a cyclical high and need your money within twelve to eighteen months? Will the market have fully recovered by then, will you have achieved your original target? *When you invest, there are no guarantees.*

Another reason to set time frames: the longer the time frame, the better your chances of achieving a *growth-*oriented objective (cf. p. 22). The more capital growth you need to achieve your objective, the longer the time you will need to reasonably achieve it. If you are prepared to invest $50,000, and need it to grow to $100,000 in three years, let me tell you something: You have a major problem!

Seriously, don't be fooled by the decade of the 80s. It was a period of time when even dart throwers could achieve 15–20 percent annualized returns. As I said earlier, it was a decade when luck was mistaken for talent. But, bottom line, it was an anomaly. Longer term, stocks, on average, return on the order of 9 percent, bonds 6–7 percent, and cash equivalents less than that. Double-digit money market rates for an extended period in the 70s and double-digit equity returns in the 80s lulled us to sleep. But not for long! Hopefully, the shock waves of more recent years have brought our feet back down to earth. If you need substantial growth, you need substantial time in which to achieve it!

Psyche

What is your stomach for risk? By now it should be clear to you that the more growth your portfolio is structured to achieve, the larger the losses you will incur during market declines.

Risk/reward is a quid pro quo equation. The more risk (capital loss), the more reward (capital gains). And vice versa.

So take a good hard look in the mirror and be honest with yourself! If the market declines 30 percent, and your portfolio drops 20 percent in value, will you be able to stay the course? Your inclination, of course, will be to cash in your remaining chips. That's why most investors lose money: they sell out at the bottom when the heat in the kitchen is hottest and buy in at the top when unbridled enthusiasm reigns.

What if your portfolio in those same circumstances was down 15 percent, or 10 percent? Will you not panic? If you cannot live with any losses at all, don't invest in the first place! Repeat, there is *no* such thing as a guaranteed investment. It is *impossible* to achieve wealth without risk.

Look yourself in the eye. If you want to go for maximum growth, be prepared for maximum losses. Investing in tortoises will cut your losses, but if the markets are in a headlong dive, you will incur substantial losses. This might seem like shock treatment, but if you go in with unreal expectations, at some point you will be terribly hurt. Unfortunately, markets don't go straight up. So how will you react the first time your portfolio goes down 5 percent, 10 percent, or 15 percent?

That's what it's all about. Know yourself, be honest, get real! Purpose, time frame, psyche.

From many years of experience, it has become apparent to me that the objectives of most investors—individuals and institutional—fall into one of five broad categories: 1. Maximum Growth, 2. Growth, 3. Balanced, 4. Income, and 5. Maximum Yield.

Let's look at each of these in terms of general characteristics and investor profiles.

Maximum Growth

As the phrase implies, this is for an investor whose sole focus is on long-term capital gains. There is no need for the portfolio to generate current income, either at present or for the foreseeable future.

Profiles: 1. A young professional earning a reasonable salary, no family responsibilities, 20–30 earning years ahead. 2. A two-income married couple, no children or none within ten years of college, high disposable income.

The focus of such investors is clearly far into the future. As such, they can afford to seek maximized gains. Besides, with taxes being what they are, current income will create an unwanted burden and not appreciably change their lifestyle in any case.

Growth

Here, the primary focus remains on long-term capital gains. However, in this instance current income is a secondary consideration. In certain cases, such income may actually be utilized on an ongoing basis; in others, the income will be reinvested in the portfolio, but it serves as an "anchor" to tone down the risk level of the overall portfolio.

Profiles: 1. A middle-aged couple within 5–10 years of retirement with no children of college age. 2. A defined benefit-pension plan with very strong cash flow, projections show contributions for active participants far exceeding payments to retirees for many years to come.

In such cases, the emphasis may still be on growth, but either because of the psychological profile, or shorter time frames, or fiduciary responsibility, lower growth expectations must be built into the portfolio. In the profiles cited here, there is little need for current income. In case one, if this couple is among what we now dub the "middle class poor," income might actually be drawn out of the account to ease budgetary constraints or to allow a slightly more luxurious lifestyle (if a substantial investment portfolio has been built up over the years, this in turn will result in a level of current income that is significant in relation to net disposable income ex the portfolio).

3. Balanced

This is the middle-of-the-road approach. Equal emphasis is placed on long-term capital growth and current income. A 50–50 discipline, as we shall see a bit later. Never a strong bet in either direction, towards growth or towards income.

Profiles: 1. Investors with only three-to-five years before their capital is needed, who must reduce their risk profile even further. 2. Those who need current income to play a

---

Food for Thought!

Historically, those who perceived themselves to be extremely conservative investors considered a portfolio concentrated in fixed income instruments to match their profile. Today, I believe this is a misconception. In recent years bonds have been almost as volatile as stocks, due to rapid shifts in interest rates. The fact that a bond provides slightly more current income than a stock is small solace indeed, particularly when capital losses might easily exceed income (i.e., negative total return). To me, the most conservative portfolio mix of all is the balanced approach, with nary a tilt to either stocks or bonds.

more important role in their financial scheme. 3. The majority of pension plans—corporate, public employee, union.

Income

The primary focus is on current income. Secondary emphasis is on capital appreciation. There is a clear need to supplement income from other sources with income from the investment portfolio. However, there is still a strong need for capital growth.

Profiles: 1. Newly retired people. While current income is clearly of paramount importance, with life expectancies being what they are today, long-term capital growth is also important in order to protect the purchasing power of the principal. 2. Those within three years of their target. Income-oriented investments have lower year-to-year volatility than growth-oriented investments. This is a way of segueing the portfolio into how it will likely look at target date. 3. Defined benefit-welfare plans (health, annuity, supplemental income, etc.). The primary emphasis *must* be on income, but not to the exclusion of growth.

Maximum Yield

The sole concern is to generate current income. No emphasis at all on the ability of the portfolio to generate long-term capital gains. Time frames are extremely short term.

Profiles: 1. Elderly people. This is a "widows and orphans" objective. Meeting day-to-day budgetary needs would be impossible without the high level of income being generated by the investment portfolio. With the exception of the "elderly optimist" (an 80-year-old who purchases a condominium in a retirement community and takes out a 30-year mortgage), there is little concern for the state of the portfolio ten-plus years from now. 2. Corporation or union retirement plans in poor financial condition: those with more retirees than active participants, or in industries with less than stellar prospects, etc. Short-term volatility could prove terminal (true, the losses in bonds in the spring of 1987 almost equaled those of stocks in October of that year, but sharp short-term swings in value occur much more frequently in stocks than in bonds). 3. Those with little stomach for risk. They probably should be in a balanced portfolio, but it will be difficult to convince them of this.

This is a snapshot of objective setting with some basic profiles. As with many aspects of the investment process, objective setting is much more an art than a science. I have seen many attempts to quantify the process (points scored for different psychoprofile questions: "I could live with a 5 percent loss for two consecutive quarters," "I need current income of 5% +/−1%," etc.), but in the end what it boils down to is gut feeling. Slotting yourself cannot be precise, at best it is a rough guideline that can be fine-tuned over time or as conditions dictate.

The profiles above were in a sense a form of guideline. Let's recap them to help you along with the process: Maximum Growth = MG, Growth = G, Balanced = B, Income = I, Maximum Yield = MY.

1. Time frames in excess of ten years: MG, G, B.
2. Time frames of five–ten years: MG, G, B, I.
3. Time frames of three–five years: G, B, I, MY.
4. Time frames under three years: B, I, MY.
5. No full-year losses in excess of 5%: MY, I, B.
6. No full-year losses in excess of 10%: MY, I, B, G.
7. Very strong need for current income: MY, I.

8. Current income nice, but not critical: I, B, G.
9. Current income of no concern: B, G, MG.

When push comes to shove, you and you alone, free of all outside influences, will know what investment posture is best. No one knows you as well as yourself. True, some individuals might be in a position to assist you with the process (unlikely if they are trying to sell you something, in which case they will try to convince you that your square peg is just right for their round hole), but in the end it will be you who makes the call. *Bottom line: This is the most critical step of all!*

The two steps that follow, Asset/sector allocation and fund selection, must conform to the predefined objective. But the wrong objective for your needs or psyche will invalidate any allocation and selection. So sweat it out, but get it right.

ASSET/SECTOR ALLOCATION

Before 1987 if you mentioned "asset allocation" to someone, you likely would have received a blank stare in return. Except among the upper reaches of institutional investors who had been using sophisticated asset allocation models for years, very few had concerned themselves with the necessity for this critical step. Conservative investors concentrated their investments in bonds; growth investors, in stocks. That's all there was to it. But as we pointed out in Chapter 3, asset class risk is a ticking time bomb just waiting to go off.

And it did—twice—in the single year of 1987. The tale is worth retelling. An interest rate spike in the spring wiped out bond investors. The October crash did the same for stock investors. Let's say it one more time: Never put all your eggs in one basket!

So step two in the building of a bulletproof portfolio is to incorporate into the portfolio the safeguards that result from good asset and sector diversification (I will explain shortly what is meant by sector diversification). The result: a portfolio with much less volatility, a means of getting off the proverbial roller coaster. Remember 1987; burn it into your mind. While bonds were collapsing in the spring, stocks were rising sharply. In the fall when stocks were collapsing, bonds were rising sharply. If you had performed asset allocation during that fateful year, you experienced much less volatility in your month-to-month and quarter-to-quarter valuations.

The next step, then, is to define which asset classes belong in the portfolio and what asset allocation method to use.

1. *No prescribed number.* No one has yet discovered the magic number of asset classes that is exactly right. Two, three, five, seven—take your pick. What we do know, as we shall explore further in point (3) below, is that if you are simply adding asset classes for the sole purpose of adding additional classes, you have accomplished nothing.

2. *Each must make economic sense.* Czarist bonds might have an investment attraction to some, but short of their potential value as a collectible, there is little to recommend their inclusion in a bulletproof portfolio. Before deluding yourself into thinking you have a well-diversified portfolio with respect to asset classes, make sure each stands on strong economic ground—that it has a reasonable chance of providing some degree of investment return, however large or small.

This is *not* a manifesto against speculation. If you feel comfortable taking the risks associated with "high flyers" such as raw land, venture capital, and others of that ilk,

Indexing

Question: What about this other buzzword you are hearing so much about—indexing? Isn't that a way to reduce wide swings in valuations? According to the theory, rather than be dependent on the substantial overperformance and underperformance that most money managers provide, you buy into a product indexed to a popular market barometer—the Dow Jones Industrial Average or the S&P 500—and assure yourself of market-like returns.

In theory (as with most investment theories) it sounds terrific. In practice, unfortunately, it doesn't work. Why? As long as the stock and bond markets suffer the degrees of turbulence from which they are currently ailing, then indexing does nothing more than assure you of market-like volatility. Case in point: If you purchased an index fund on Friday, 9 October 1987 and sold it at the close on Monday, 19 October, you suffered the same 30 percent drop the market experienced over those six days, plus that fund's daily operating expense ratio. Case in point: If you purchased a stock index fund at the close on Thursday, 12 October 1989 and sold it one day later, you suffered the same 6.1 percent one-day decline as the market, plus 0.1 or 0.2 percent in operating expenses. To put it succinctly: Indexing keeps you on the roller coaster. It does nothing to get you off it.

fine. High risk/high reward. That's fine. As a high-risk player, they make economic sense to you. That's what counts.

3. *Each asset class should react differently to various*

stimuli. In Chapter 3, I made the point that securities within a given asset class normally react similarly to the same stimuli. Now let's look at the flip side: true asset class diversification is achieved when each class in your portfolio reacts differently to the same stimuli.

Examples: A weakening economy is generally not favorable for stocks (lower corporate earnings, fewer dividend increases, etc.), but it is a good environment for bonds (as the economy slows, the Federal Reserve Board normally takes steps to stimulate the economy—lowering interest rates, increasing money supply). During periods of high inflation, gold as a rule does well, but stocks do poorly. In periods of low inflation, stocks do well, real estate less so.

So, if you want a portfolio that can ride out virtually any storm with as little buffeting as possible, with the ability to minimize losses (the eventual road to success), have a portfolio spread across asset classes in which at least one or more will always be appreciating.

4. *Miscellaneous asset classes.* The purview of this book is stocks, bonds, and money market instruments. That does not preclude the use of other asset classes: oil and gas, real estate (see item 6 below), art and other collectibles, gold (more on that in a moment), venture capital, etc. as long as they conform to the three preceding guidelines. Remember also we are in the second stage of portfolio development. Stage one—objective setting—already set down an additional qualification: "Know thyself"; don't believe you need one of these miscellaneous assets in your portfolio simply because someone tells you so, or because it's currently in vogue. If its voguish, you'll probably be one of the last in and one of the last out.

5. *Gold.* How do you define a commodity whose price might be determined by the accuracy of a madman firing at the president of the United States? That's gold. Yet it is universally recognized as a store of value, perhaps the ulti-

mate store. Companies fail, currencies are devalued and debased, but gold is eternal.

I recall a friend, a well-established businessman, who on a regular basis (pre-perestroika) accumulated gold certificates backed by gold stored in Switzerland. Why? As an insurance policy against the day when hammer and sickle might be flying over the White House. I could argue with him until I was blue in the face but there was no reasoning with him.

But perhaps that's what gold truly is, an investment without reason. Universally accepted, but on what basis? Fear, psychic well-being, insurance. In this latter respect alone, there seems to be some rationale—not in the terms expressed by my friend, but rather as an insurance policy against hyperinflation. *None* of the investments mentioned above works well in periods of hyperinflation. Yet such periods are few and far between, particularly in this country. Many less-developed countries in recent years have faced periods of inflation rising by 1 percent per day or more. In the Weimar Republic of post–World War I Germany wheelbarrows of currency were required to buy a loaf of bread. In the United States, we have been spared such situations.

But if you fear such an occurrence, then as part of your total financial plan, not an investment plan, you should own gold. Fearful of your mortality, you purchase life insurance. Fearful of hyperinflation, you purchase gold. You don't fix a monthly or quarterly value on your life insurance and measure its performance. Neither should you track the month-by-month or quarter-by-quarter changes in price of gold and measure its performance. In the final analysis, *gold is an insurance policy, not an investment.*

6. *Real estate.* Real estate is an investment, but one that is very difficult to handle. It is characterized by a total lack of liquidity, is completely subject to supply and demand,

and is truly long term in nature. It is an asset, but one which requires many layers of diversification if it is to work successfully as an investment.

You need a broad cross-section of properties, spread across many different geographical markets, diversified by type (office buildings, shopping centers, apartment houses, etc.) and by managers. I have never heard of a single manager adept in a variety of markets and with different types of properties.

With that as background, real estate does have a place in your portfolio. Generally, it is an asset class that will work well for you in periods of moderate inflation. Rent increases and the prices of underlying properties keep up well in such an environment, but remember: diversify, diversify, diversify.

Methods of Asset Allocation

Next, we must conduct a brief overview of the four main methods of asset allocation. We will identify their major characteristics, their pros and cons, and most importantly, how much effort and expertise each requires. Here they are: 1. Fully invested, 2. Fixed mix, 3. Active asset allocation, and 4. Market timing.

Fully Invested (a.k.a. Buy-and-Hold). Actually, this is anti–asset allocation. Proponents would say as follows:

The Ibbotson studies (see pp. 21–23) show conclusively that the best inflation fighter long term is stocks. I am a true long-term investor and am willing to look beyond all the shorter-term valleys in order to get to the far off peaks. Stocks provide an average annual return over the long term far superior to that provided by both bonds and money market instruments. Why allocate? Would my returns be superior if at times—particularly when equity markets are slumping—I stayed out of the market? Obviously yes, but I don't believe anybody can consistently call market turns. I would rather be in all the time.

This monologue is not all that hypothetical. It is almost verbatim the credo of Peter Lynch when he ran the Fidelity Magellan Fund and has been the operating philosophy of many a successful investor. Don't waste your time asset allocating. Don't trouble yourself over what percentage of your assets should be in cash. Definitely don't fritter away valuable time timing the market. Assemble a good portfolio of stocks, upgrade it as need be by trimming off the weeds (the weak performers that you don't believe will bounce back) and add new promising names as they come to your attention. Or, buy one or more well-managed tortoise stock funds. There's a great deal that can be said in favor of this alternative, but let's carefully study its pros and cons.

Pros: There is no chance of being "whipsawed," being in the wrong place at the wrong time. You build up bond positions just prior to a spike up in rates; you sell off stocks days before a major stock market rally. This a major danger of market timing in particular and active allocation to a lesser extent. Not to mention the increased trading costs associated with each in-and-out move and the larger than necessary actual losses (or, at best, opportunity costs).

Assuming you stay for the long term, you should capture the historically superior returns afforded by equities. If you first invest at a market high (i.e., August 1987), it might take quite a while to hit the desired 9–10 percent annualized level. But history says eventually you will be rewarded.

Con: You need a cast-iron stomach! I sound like a broken record, but if you had invested at the 1987 market high near 2700 in late summer, and two months later saw your portfolio down 37 percent (assuming your portfolio did no worse than the market), would you stay the course? Could you truly say to yourself that you have the resolve to look past some valleys to the distant peaks (which from your perspective at the very bottom of the valley may not even be visible)? Remember, step one of building a portfolio revolved on the theme "know thyself." Take a good look in the mirror. Could you stay the course if, for instance, you began investing in the beginning of 1973, suffered a 40–80 percent loss over the next 21 months (depending on how aggressive a growth fund you owned), and might have had to wait a decade simply to get back to break-even? Please, take a good long look at yourself.

Buy and hold can work, but it requires an iron will. Otherwise, you will turn into that most typical investors— the one who gets swept up by euphoria and buys in at market highs, then loses faith at the very bottom and sells out. There's a ready formula for failure: buy high; sell low.

Fixed Mix. This is asset allocation for those who believe in the basic concept, but do not have the time, inclination or expertise to put it into practice on an ongoing basis. The answer? Decide on a blend that makes sense to you, that fits rather closely with your objective, put it into place and leave it alone. Perhaps quarterly, semiannually, or once a year you readjust the portfolio to its original configuration. For instance, say that you had put 40% into growth funds, 40% into bond funds, and 20% into money market funds. Then, after a year, due to market action the growth funds now equaled 50% of your assets, bond funds, 35%, and money market funds, 15%. You would sell 10% of your total in growth funds and redeploy the proceeds equally into your bond funds and money market funds. You're now back to 40–40–20.

Let's look at the pros and cons of this halfway step:

Pros: This is definitely a time saver. In effect you are doing it once and putting it away.

Fixed mix probably makes sense for those with limited training or research resources at their disposal. If not prepared to perform active asset allocation yourself nor to rely on the recommendations provided by brokerage firms, advisory letters, or the business press, then you're better off with a fixed mix approach.

Cons: You will experience less volatility in returns than those utilizing a fully-invested approach, but considerably more than those employing an active asset allocation approach. Think about it: do you really want to be 40 percent in stocks all the time? 40 percent in bonds?

Everything comes at a price. The price for the relative ease of fixed mix allocation is that you have a higher percentage of your portfolio in an undesirable area (even if it is only for a short period of time) than those who are actively managing their portfolios. Again, know thyself!

Active Asset Allocation. Let me ask you a question: what is traditional portfolio management? Is it not a full-time professional money manager assessing economic, monetary, and political conditions, making a judgment as to where we stand in terms of the economic and interest rate cycles, and then finally determining the proper mix of stocks, bonds, and money market instruments to fit that scenario? Doesn't that portfolio manager over the course of the economic cycle vary and fine-tune the mix of assets as their risk/reward parameters change? In modern parlance, we call it active asset allocation. To me, it is nothing more than traditional portfolio management.

This description, therefore, aptly describes the third form of asset allocation. The investor, either by self-determination or by reliance upon external sources, will make a judgment concerning the relative merits of different asset classes. As we move along the economic cycle, those relative merits change. Stocks are a much more attractive asset early in the recovery phase than as we approach a recession. Conversely, bonds early in a recovery—when interest rates would normally be rising due to business demand—are generally less attractive than as we enter a recession, when the Federal Reserve would normally be lowering interest rates in an attempt to stimulate a sluggish economy.

To keep the portfolio in line with the changing scenario, the investor will make small changes in asset allocation, as I described it a moment ago: fine-tuning. The investment environment changes in small, gradual steps; so should your asset allocation—perhaps reallocation of no more than 5–10 percent at a time. True, interest rates may rise sharply and stock markets may fall precipitously, but that normally is a reflection of the marketplace "catching up" to reality.

Reality, fundamentals. Arguments rage over the relative merits of technical analysis versus fundamental analysis, but my money is on the latter (more on technical analysis in a moment, when we discuss market timing). How does that expression go, "Those who cannot remember the past are condemned to repeat it?" How true, how true!

Graph all historical data relating to price/earnings ratios, price/book value, price/yield, and stock yields vs. bond yields. Break this data down into deciles. How often do you think the stock market rises after current prices push the market into the ninth or tenth decile of historical overvaluation? Right, not very often. Yet by fundamental standards the market by early 1987 was grossly overvalued. By active asset allocation, you would have been gradually reducing your equity exposure throughout the spring and summer of that year as the market continued to rise ("selling into strength"). Yes, the rally continued on until August—isn't it amazing how far euphoria can carry a market—but then reality caught up with it.

We had a repeat performance in 1989 and the first half of 1990. Clearly, the economic recovery was on its last legs. In terms of time, it was one of the longest in the postwar period. Market valuations once again entered the ninth and tenth deciles of historical overvaluation. Yet the market rose over 30 percent in 1989, culminating with a close just shy of 3000 (2999.75) in the summer of 1990. Again, active asset allocation could have been gradually stepping out throughout this span of time, and once again the market "caught up" with a mighty thud.

Active asset allocation in this sense is also a tortoise approach—slow but steady, with gradual shifts around basic guidelines dictated by one's investment objectives. (Later we shall look more closely at parameters and different mixes for different scenarios.) Such shifts will be dictated either by changes in the investment environment as described above, or by fixed mix allocation, where the performance for one asset class has so skewed the relative allocation that purchases and sales must be made to rebalance the portfolio (I suggest you wait until at least a 5 percent shift has occurred before you rebalance).

Newer forms of active asset allocation have surfaced in recent years, particularly since the October 1987 crash. "Tactical" and "strategic" asset allocation, basically computer-driven and moving in rather large increments (10–50 percent), have captured the imagination of the trendsetters. Institutional investors, stripped bare by such nonsensical new-and-different investment approaches as portfolio insurance (which, of course, failed miserably the first time it was called on to show its mettle in the Crash of '87), returned as willingly as lambs to the slaughter to be fleeced once again. Care to guess what carried the rally in 1989 through the end of the year? If your answer was asset allocators who tactically or strategically had missed the first half of the year rally because their computer models told them to stay totally out of stocks, you score 100.

To repeat: people run portfolios, not computers. And whether those computers are picking individual stocks or asset classes/allocations, *it ain't gonna work!*

Back to the basic "old-fashioned" active asset allocation. Let's examine its pluses and minuses:

Pros: 1. It allows you to keep in step with changes in the relative risk/reward characteristics of each asset class in your portfolio.

2. Unless implemented improperly, it should allow you to sidestep disasters. You are not locked in to any proportion of any asset class.

3. Because changes are done gradually in small incremental steps, the chance of getting whipsawed is diminished.

Cons: 1. This approach is time intensive. Since you will be shifting allocations over the course of cycles (economic, interest rate, stock and bond market), you must be constantly on the alert. Even if changes occur only 3–5 times a year (based on my personal experience), trends must be constantly checked.

2. Expertise is required. There is no instant way to perform active asset allocation. Either by using one's own training or by relying on those with sufficient credentials, judgments must be made on the economy, interest rates, stock market valuations, bond market levels, etc.

Market Timing.

Answer: The fountain of youth, the pot of gold at the end of the rainbow, and a successful market timing system.

Question: What three things have men always dreamed of finding?

Sorry, but that about sums it up. Virtually every independent study (Hulbert et al.) of market timing systems—particularly those that use mutual funds as a means of quick access to and exit from the market—has reached the same conclusion: most don't work, and those that do, have no consistency in their ability to predict market turns. Ergo, *mistiming.*

Conceptually, the idea is terrific. Download into a computer tons of historical data. Interest rates, corporate earnings, money supply, new highs, new lows, trading volume, etc. Track what each of these was doing at important market turns; identify those that seem to recur with the most regularity at such turns. Finally, create a model that will track these critical inputs on a going-forward basis—when they reach a certain confluence, a buy signal will be generated; at a later confluence, a sell signal is issued.

As there are no gray areas in such models, generally the signals will trigger large asset shifts (25–50–100 percent). Either you belong in stocks or you don't, the market timing proponent would say. Either you belong in bonds or you don't. There is no middle ground. Depending on the sensitivity of the model to trends, such signals may occur as often 3–5 times per year or as few as 1–2 times. Clearly there are costs to such trading (actual trading costs, plus opportunity costs—being out when you should be in, and vice versa), but if the system works, the improved returns will more than offset these costs.

Let's look at pros and cons:

Pros: If your timing system works, and that is a big if, it will shield you from disasters. Theoretically, such systems keep you out of the market during most of a decline and fully invested for the majority of time that the market is rising. Goal: capture most of the gains and avoid most of the losses.

Cons: 1. For such systems to function properly, there must be an orderliness to the market, which most often goes up when we expect it to go down, and vice versa. There is a century-old text on the psychology of mobs that many a sage investor has told me is basic reading for any would-be investor. In fact, as I write, intensive research is being undertaken into how to relate the emerging science of chaos (patterns of irregularity) to the stock market. Let me ask you: how do you time chaos?

2. As noted above, because of the rapidity with which major allocation moves are made, costs are significant. Even if no-load funds are used as the investment vehicle, thereby negating trading costs, opportunity costs may still be significant.

3. Whipsaws. When you are dealing with a roller-coaster market with rapid back-and-forth shifts such as we have had for some time now, there is a strong possibility of a reversal, at which point you "unwind" your mistake and sell just when you should be buying. Short, rapid moves of 5–10 percent in either direction (enough to trigger most any timing system) are more and more becoming the norm rather than the exception.

Each investor, after careful self-examination, will have to determine which of these four approaches to asset allocation is right for them. If your sole consideration in choosing between these four main avenues is the amount of time you can devote to your investments, perhaps the following Effort Meter will put it in perspective:

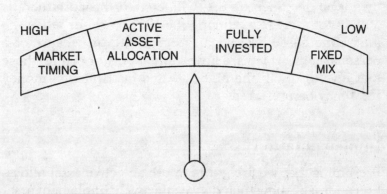

My own tastes, in order of preference, are as follows: 1. active asset allocation, 2. fixed mix, 3. fully invested, and 4. market timing.

Sector Allocation

Sector allocation is the second half of asset allocation. It is a refinement of the allocation process. If asset allocation is viewed as setting the broad-brush outlines of your portfolio, then sector allocation is the adding of detail to the picture. Look upon it in the following terms:

ALLOCATIONS

Asset:		Growth	
Sector:	Aggressive		Conservative
Asset:		Income	
Sector:	Equity		Fixed
	Equity-income		High/Low Grade
	Growth & income		Long/Intermediate/Short
	Balanced		Governments/Corporates
Asset:		Cash	
Sector:	Government Only	Prime	General

To me, a money market fund is a money market fund is a money market fund. In other words, go for the highest yield available. But to some, whether because it is dictated by a legal document (trust, will, etc.), or because there is a flight to safety (e.g., during the 1987 crash, or when the junk bond fiasco first began to unwind), or because of a personal comfort level, a government-only or prime (those that invest only in the highest rated instruments) money fund may be preferred.

Implementation

Presuming that we are going to use an active asset allocation approach, how then do we effectively implement asset and sector allocation? A few ground rules are in order, regardless of your objectives:

Do it gradually. As I said earlier, under normal conditions, shift 5 percent of your portfolio to adjust it to where you want it to be.

Do whatever makes you comfortable. Remember, asset/sector allocations are an offshoot of objective setting. As step one must leave you with a sense of comfort, so must step two (and so must step three—mutual fund selection).

If you're doing it often, you're probably doing it too often.

True, the world is changing more rapidly, but not to such a degree that requires you to implement changes in asset/ sector allocation on a weekly, monthly, or quarterly basis. Based on over fifteen years' experience, on average a total of 15–20 percent over the course of the year should be sufficient fine-tuning to have your portfolio where you want it to be.

Rapid shifts in events call for rapid shifts in allocations. This is the converse of the first rule. That is the norm; this is the exception. Let's get specific. During the day of 19 October 1987 I met with my investment policy committee on three separate occasions. By the end of the first hour of trading, we had already decided to move 5 percent back into the market (conservative growth) out of cash holdings, which stood at 30 percent at the beginning of the day. By early afternoon, as the decline accelerated, we met again and decided to add a further 5 percent to the amount we were prepared to recommit to the market. Later in the afternoon, when the market was down a total of 22 percent on the day, we decided to up the total going back into conservative growth funds to 15 percent.

This really wasn't a negation of the first rule. We made three gradual shifts, each of which was intended as a means of buying into weakness; the speed with which events unfolded caused all three of these steps to occur on a single day. The 12–19th of October, or more precisely 19 October as the culmination of a 30 percent crash over six trading days, was a one-day bear market. Under more normal conditions, we would have reached the same three conclusions, but over a longer time span.

Discipline

Asset/sector allocation can be a free-form, spur of the moment process—what is often called flying by the seat of your pants. On the other hand, allocations can be, actually should be, made in a disciplined, well-thought-out fashion.

Discipline—it's a word I've heard used over and over again by the most successful investors and portfolio managers. It defines every blueprint for success. Look at the helter-skelter investment world of today and recall the old adage: "If you can keep your head while all those around you are losing theirs . . ." Discipline is the key to every stage of successful portfolio construction—objective setting, asset/sector allocation, tortoise fund selection (and to stock and bond selection by those funds' managers). In my estimation, though, it is never as critical as in allocation.

Let's look at two aspects of allocation discipline: bands and moving targets. As we discuss each of these, please remember that they are merely guidelines. They are not etched in stone. They are reference points to guide you along the course of market and economic cycles. Extraordinary circumstances require extraordinary measures. These numbers are not sacrosanct; they can be adjusted. In other words, *do not confuse discipline with rigidity,* or calcification between the ears, as I prefer to call it.

Bands. I earlier identified five objectives which experience has shown me apply to over 90 percent of investors: maximum growth, growth, balanced, income and maximum yield. I then defined (p. 138) five major asset-sectors: aggressive growth, conservative growth, equity income, fixed income and money market. These two sets become the vertical and horizontal axes for our bands in Table 8.1.

What we will do is to set limits, minimum and maximum, for each asset-sector for each type of investor. To wit, how much do you want to own of each of these asset-sectors in a worst-case situation and a best-case situation?

Let's look at these parameters a bit more closely. Start with the most growth-oriented investor: maximum growth. The data below indicates that in the most bullish of scenarios, such an investor would probably want to

TABLE 8.1

Asset-Sector Allocation Bands

Objective	Aggressive Growth	Conservative Growth	Equity Income	Fixed Income	Money Market
Maximum Growth	20–70%	15–50%	0–30%	0–30%	0–5 %
Growth	15–40	15–45	10–30	10–40	0–50
Balanced	10–30	10–40	15–40	15–60	0–50
Income	0–10	0–30	10–40	30–80	0–50
Maximum Yield	0	0	10–30	40–90	0–50

have as much as 70 percent of total assets in aggressive growth funds, a lesser amount in conservative growth funds, and an even smaller amount in equity income, fixed income, and money market funds. By contrast, to move completely across the spectrum, maximum yield investors should probably never have any portion of their portfolios in aggressive growth or conservative growth funds. However, taking cognizance of asset risk and therefore never wanting to be 100% in bonds, such an investor should always have at least 10% in equity income funds and might at times have as much as 30% in this category. (Equity exposure in such an instance will not actually total 30% since funds in this category—equity income/growth and income/balanced—will generally have a percentage of their portfolios in bonds and cash.)

The same holds true for the other three objectives as well. These bands provide a discipline at the extremes. As you shift your allocations within sectors, you will be able to judge how close you are getting to the limits. For instance, Ms. Jones considers herself to be a growth investor. Having concluded that prospects are brightening for corporate earnings, she shifts assets out of money market funds into conservative growth funds. Her portfolio now looks like this: 35% aggressive growth, 40% conservative growth, 10% equity income, 10% fixed income, 5% money market.

Question: Ms. Jones, you are within 5 percent of your upper limits for both aggressive growth and conservative growth funds. Do you really think we are that close to an optimum environment for stocks? Do you really want to be that bullish?

Ms. Jones might respond that only 75 percent of her total assets are in growth funds and as such she is not that bullish. Wrong, Ms. Jones! Since because of asset risk you would never allow yourself to be 100 percent in growth funds, in actuality you are within 10% of the maximum (40% + 45%) that your allocation discipline will allow you for growth funds. That's what bands are all about.

Moving targets. Bands provide us with the minimum and maximum we should allocate to each asset-sector for various objectives. That is one sort of discipline. Moving targets constitute another. Here's how they work.

Since we are dealing with situations that are cyclical in nature (interest rate cycles, economic cycles, etc.), we want to create for ourselves a series of reference points along the continuum to make sure our current allocation makes sense. "I feel slightly bullish. This is what my portfolio currently looks like. How does that compare with where I said I wanted to be at this point in the cycle?"

To set up our moving targets, I will once again fall back on the magic five—five targets for five objectives invested in five asset-sectors. Here are the targets: very bullish, bullish, neutral, bearish, very bearish. Obviously, we could create many more targets, but in the interest of KISS (Keep It Simple, Stupid) these five should suffice.

Warning: When we talk of "bearish" and "bullish," we mean in terms of the environment for stocks. Generally, what is good for stocks is not good for bonds, as I have pointed out a number of times. Therefore, when we set up allocations in a very bullish environment, it will assume a favorable atmosphere for growth-oriented investors and a negative atmosphere for income-oriented investors. However, there were extended periods of time throughout the 70s and 80s when stocks and bonds moved in the same direction. Clearly an anomaly, but a reality just the same. If this should recur, then "very bullish" and "bullish" will mean the same for both growth and income investors. To repeat, moving targets are reference points; they are not chiseled in stone.

How does one go about setting up targets? I have found the best way is to work from the middle outwards. In other words, start with your neutral scenario—when you don't have strong feelings in either direction—then bullish and bearish, and finally very bullish and very bearish. Why? Because as in any good game plan, the center is the core, the anchor. This is what your portfolio should look like on a level plane. Next, see how it looks when we tilt it a little bit in one direction or the other. Last, see how it would look when tilted to the maximum to which we will allow it to go (remember the bands). You simply couldn't follow that logical progression working from the outside in. Table 8.2 shows my suggestion for asset/sector allocation in a neutral situation.

TABLE 8.2

Asset/Sector Allocation, Neutral

Objective	Aggressive Growth	Conservative Growth	Equity Income	Fixed Income	Money Market
Maximum Growth	40%	20%	10%	20%	10%
Growth	20	25	20	25	10
Balanced	15	20	25	30	10
Income	5	15	20	50	10
Maximum Yield	0	0	20	70	10

There is a great deal to chew on here. Let's first look at this matrix in reference to objective. A good bogey or benchmark against which to measure a maximum growth portfolio would be 70% equity/30% debt. Hence, our maximum growth allocation has 70% of total assets in growth funds, with the largest concentration in aggressive growth funds. A bogey for a growth account would be 65/35; our growth allocation has 65% in growth funds; largest concentration: conservative growth. Balanced bogey: 60/40; allocation: 60% growth funds; largest concentration: equity income. Income bogey: 40/60; allocation: 40% growth funds; largest concentration: equity income. Maximum yield bogey: 20/80; allocation: 20% growth funds; largest concentration: fixed income.

Which means that when you are in a neutral position, when you don't have strong inclinations in either direction, your portfolio should be indexed to the benchmark against which you are measuring performance on a relative basis. Put another way—a benchmark is fixed; it does not move around as your sentiments change. So, for instance, if you grew bullish, you would want a higher concentration in growth funds than the bogey has. That's how you can gauge if your allocation 'bet' paid off. Did you achieve a higher rate of return by adding to growth than the benchmarks achieved with its "fixed mix"? When you are neutral, you are not placing any bets. Ergo, your allocation should match that of the bogey.

As long as I referred to fixed mix, let me point out one other factor. If you do not feel inclined to indulge in active asset allocation and therefore prefer a fixed mix approach, the allocations set forth above for a neutral scenario can serve as your allocation. Again, it reflects a portfolio mix in which you are not prepared to tilt the allocations in either direction, which is *exactly* the definition of a fixed mix investor.

One last piece of analysis of Table 8.2. Look at it from a

vertical perspective. The allocation to aggressive growth shrinks from top to bottom; the allocation to fixed income shrinks from bottom to top. Both of these factors can help you understand which objective is right for you (Know thyself). The ability to absorb risk and the stomach for fluctuations in portfolio values climbs as we go up the ladder. The need for income and the desire for greater stability grows greater as we climb down the ladder.

Time to move on. We now take one step out in either direction away from dead center. Table 8.3 shows what happens to allocations when you grow somewhat bullish.

What has occurred here? The environment has shifted in favor of equities, and so has our allocation. The maximum growth and growth investors are more adventuresome, shifting 10 percent (maximum growth, as would be expected, into aggressive growth funds; growth investors equally into aggressive growth and conservative growth funds). The more conservative balanced, income, and maximum yield investors shift a mere 5 percent (balanced now "balances" the allocation to conservative growth—the beneficiary of the shift—and equity income, while the income and maximum yield investors opt for the more conservative equity income funds).

The source of assets for this shift? Reductions in the

TABLE 8.3

Asset/Sector Allocation, Bullish

Objective	Aggressive Growth	Conservative Growth	Equity Income	Fixed Income	Money Market
Maximum Growth	50%	25%	5%	10%	10%
Growth	25	30	20	15	10
Balanced	15	25	25	25	10
Income	5	15	25	45	10
Maximum Yield	0	0	25	65	10

allocations to fixed income funds. Why? Broken record time: What's good for stocks is generally not good for bonds. Let's assume the economy is heating up. Corporate earnings rising, leading indicators up, unemployment down, plant utilization climbing. Clearly a time when you want to favor growth in your portfolio, but what also happens in such an environment? Interest rates rise either because of stronger business demand for credit or because the Federal Reserve fears runaway growth/inflation and decides to tighten the screws a bit.

Even income-oriented investors (balanced, income, maximum yield) must cut their allocations to fixed income in such a scenario, because *as rates rise capital losses will more than offset any incremental gain in yield. Remember, we are interested in the bottom line, or total return.* TOTAL RETURN = INCOME + CAPITAL GAINS/LOSSES. If by not reducing your bond fund allocation in a rising interest rate environment you increased income by 1%, but suffered a 2% capital loss, then you won the battle but lost the war. Besides, by shifting into the equity income sector—which is comprised of growth and income, equity-income, and balanced funds, all of which generally favor higher-dividend-paying stocks—the drop in current income on a portfolio-wide basis will be minimal.

Now, let's look at a slight tilt in the opposite direction (Table 8.4).

As you can see, this is a virtually mirror image of the bullish scenario. Now, the outlook for equities is disappointing. Corporate earnings are slowing and overall there is much less zest in the economy. Stock prices might still rise but at a decidedly slower pace than in the past.

The result: maximum growth and growth investors pull a net 10 percent out of their growth fund holdings. The former cut their exposure to aggressive growth funds; the latter equally to aggressive and conservative growth. Balanced, income, and maximum yield investors, with less

TABLE 8.4

Asset/Sector Allocation, Bearish

Objective	Aggressive Growth	Conservative Growth	Equity Income	Fixed Income	Money Market
Maximum Growth	30%	15%	15%	30%	10%
Growth	15	20	20	35	10
Balanced	10	20	25	35	10
Income	0	15	20	55	10
Maximum Yield	0	0	15	75	10

exposure to growth funds to begin with, pare back 5 percent. The two former groups take assets from their aggressive growth holdings; maximum yield from its sole equity exposure—equity income funds.

Where do these assets shift to? Correct, bond funds. If the economy is slowing, there is less demand for credit and rates will generally be declining. Ergo, lower yields on bond funds, but significant capital appreciation. This also explains the attractiveness at this point of bond funds over money market funds. With rates falling, probably at the short end of the interest rate curve as well, cash funds provide a lower return.

Now we go further out along the spectrum (Table 8.5).

Both maximum growth and growth investors take advantage of an extremely advantageous environment for equities: the onset of an economic recovery—coming out of a recession, leading indicators sharply up, unemployment sharply lower. These investors will make major commitments to growth funds (more so by the maximum growth investor, of course). Even balanced and income investors take the plunge, but in a much more conservative way. Their use of equity income funds matches their exposure to aggressive and conservative growth funds, growth-oriented but conservatively. With 70% of assets in equity

TABLE 8.5

Asset/Sector Allocation, Very Bullish

Objective	Aggressive Growth	Conservative Growth	Equity Income	Fixed Income	Money Market
Maximum Growth	60%	30%	0%	5%	5%
Growth	35	35	10	10	10
Balanced	25	30	20	15	10
Income	10	20	25	30	15
Maximum Yield	0	0	30	55	15

income/bond/money market funds, the income investor can still generate a fair level of income with such a mix. The shortfall precipitated by a 15% drop in the allocation to fixed income funds will be partially offset by a slightly higher allocation to money market funds, and higher short-term rates. Remember, one tool the Federal Reserve can use to keep the reins on a booming economy is to tighten up on rates. We have seen this at the latter stages of the first leg of each recovery in the postwar period, most recently in 1983.

For this reason, the source of assets for our increased commitments to growth funds comes once again from bond funds. Rates are rising, but don't be tempted to nibble just yet. They may rise higher until the Fed sees that its plan has worked—that the economy has slowed down somewhat. What to look for: quarter-to-quarter and year-to-year percentage growth in the gross national product (GNP) lower than in the prior quarter, perhaps the prior two quarters. That will be an indication that both the Federal Reserve board of governors and yourself can take as a clear sign that more reasonable growth (not overheated or highly inflationary) lies ahead. *That* is when you can start playing around with the higher rates then available.

Then to the flip side, the situation we as investors never want to face, but real all the same (Table 8.6).

A recession is clearly in the offing. Unemployment is soaring, corporate profits are plunging, the Fed is using all the tools at its disposal to get money back into the system (reduced Fed funds rates, cuts in the discount rate, etc.). Economic activity in general is slowing.

This is when you want to pull your horns in. A low, low profile in the stock market, a high profile in the bond market. Reasonable money market reserves to be used as a safe haven and buying reserve. Profits may still be achieved, but in all likelihood they will now emanate from the fixed income portion of the portfolio. (Example: If interest rates begin the year at 10%, and over the course of the year rates fall to 9%, for the full year, you will have earned 10% in current income and approximately 10% in capital appreciation—a bond with a 10% coupon is worth 10% more than one with a 9% coupon—for a total return of approximately 20%.)

Since we are not market timers, maximum growth and growth investors will keep only minimal exposure to growth funds. On the other hand, income-oriented investors (income and maximum yield) will have built up siz-

TABLE 8.6

Asset/Sector Allocation, Very Bearish

Objective	Aggressive Growth	Conservative Growth	Equity Income	Fixed Income	Money Market
Maximum Growth	20%	15%	15%	35%	15%
Growth	15	15	10	45	15
Balanced	10	10	15	50	15
Income	0	5	10	65	20
Maximum Yield	0	0	10	80	10

able bond positions to benefit from the potential capital appreciation opportunity in bonds and a still relatively attractive yield. If rates and stock prices bottom out—at which point the yield on stocks may prove quite attractive relative to the reduced yield on bonds—then such investors will look more and more towards stocks as an income source and less towards bonds. *Income is income, regardless of whether you get it from stocks, bonds, or money market instruments!*

One final point: You may have noticed that in many instances in developing moving targets, we did not reach the extreme of our bands. For example, in our very bullish scenario, we did not have 70% in aggressive growth funds for maximum growth investors; nor did we have 90% in fixed income funds for maximum yield investors in our very bearish scenario. The reason for this is simple: Those extremes are held in reserve for exceptional circumstances. Thus, a maximum growth investor in a normal very bullish scenario is clearly well represented in growth funds with a combined 90% (60 + 30) of assets in aggressive and conservative growth funds. But if it becomes evident that this is an environment where sharp premiums are being paid for small-cap, emerging growth stocks (which is the type of issue you are more likely to find in aggressive growth fund portfolios than conservative growth funds), you may keep the total exposure to growth funds at 90%, but now have 70% in aggressive growth funds and 20% in conservative growth funds.

Tip: How can you tell when premiums are being paid for such stocks? First, check the performance of the Russell 2000—a barometer of smaller capitalization issues—versus the Russell 1000—higher cap stocks. Then check the performance of the NASDAQ Index—emerging growth stocks—versus the S&P 500—established growth stocks. If either of these excel consistently for a period of three to four months, that should warrant switching your mix. In the case of the maximum yield investor, the same holds true. If plant utilization percentages are falling off the cliff, if the tilt turns from mild inflation to deflation, if fears are intensifying that we might be headed for a very deep recession (or even a depression), then this investor would want even more assets in fixed income funds. *Bottom line: Save the extremes of the bands for extreme situations.*

The best way of recapping the concept of moving targets is to chart them now according to each objective (Tables 8.7–11).

What is obvious as we survey the array of allocations in Tables 8.7–8.11 is the symmetry of the process—regular

TABLE 8.7

Maximum Growth

Scenario	Aggressive Growth	Conservative Growth	Equity Income	Fixed Income	Money Market
Very Bullish	60%	30%	0%	5%	5%
Bullish	50	25	5	10	10
Neutral	40	20	10	20	10
Bearish	30	15	15	30	10
Very Bearish	20	15	15	35	15

TABLE 8.8

Growth

Scenario	Aggressive Growth	Conservative Growth	Equity Income	Fixed Income	Money Market
Very Bullish	35%	35%	10%	10%	10%
Bullish	25	30	20	15	10
Neutral	20	25	20	25	10
Bearish	15	20	20	35	10
Very Bearish	15	15	10	45	15

TABLE 8.9

Balanced

Scenario	Aggressive Growth	Conservative Growth	Equity Income	Fixed Income	Money Market
Very Bullish	25%	30%	20%	15%	10%
Bullish	15	25	25	25	10
Neutral	15	20	25	30	10
Bearish	10	20	25	35	10
Very Bearish	10	10	15	50	15

TABLE 8.10

Income

Scenario	Aggressive Growth	Conservative Growth	Equity Income	Fixed Income	Money Market
Very Bullish	10%	20%	25%	30%	15%
Bullish	5	15	25	45	10
Neutral	5	15	20	50	10
Bearish	0	15	20	55	10
Very Bearish	0	5	10	65	20

TABLE 8.11

Maximum Yield

Scenario	Aggressive Growth	Conservative Growth	Equity Income	Fixed Income	Money Market
Very Bullish	0%	0%	30%	55%	15%
Bullish	0	0	25	65	10
Neutral	0	0	20	70	10
Bearish	0	0	15	75	10
Very Bearish	0	0	10	80	10

steps down in equity exposure as the economic environment softens, with "gutsier" investors (maximum growth and growth) swinging more widely. At the same time, we see regular steps up in fixed income exposure, proportionate to the decline in equity exposure. Often exposure can also be adjusted by shifting into or out of equity income funds, since the funds in this category—growth and income, balanced, equity-income—are likely to have some mix of stocks, bonds, and cash in their portfolios. A shift from equity income funds into conservative growth funds, therefore, will likely increase equity exposure in your overall portfolio.

Why, you may ask, is so little allocated to money market funds in these examples? Good question! The reason is because we were assuming normal conditions: when the economy is weakening, and interest rates would usually be declining, you can make more in bonds than in cash equivalents. When the economy is strengthening and interest rates should be rising, stocks will provide a significantly higher total rate of return than cash equivalents. In other words, cash is a buffer that will mute downside performance in negative environments. It is a reserve that can be called upon if a buying opportunity presents itself. In many respects, it is the rainy day fund within the investment portfolio. But, and this is an awfully big but, what if the economy is softening and interest rates for whatever reason do not come down? What if the economy is beginning to strengthen and stocks are not rising in price? Our world—economic, political, monetary—becomes more complex with every passing day. A barely-out-of-college computer whiz decides to implement a program trade on the futures exchange, and the stock market goes into a sudden tailspin. A commodity trader, not old enough to model for a Gillette ad, starts going long and presto, the price of oil is up 20 percent. Things simply don't always go as planned. What then? Plain and simple: Duck!

Throughout the 70s and 80s, things often did not go as planned, and so we had many, many instances of stocks and bonds moving in the same direction (even though over the longer term, dating back to the earlier part of this century, stocks and bonds have moved in the same direction less than 20 percent of the time). *When the direction they are both going in is down, you want to be in cash.* That is why in developing bands, I allowed up to 50 percent in money market funds for each of the five objectives. Get to the sidelines and wait for the dust to settle.

Similarly, if both stocks and bonds are rising in value and you're getting a bit nervous that this can't go on forever, perhaps it's time to take some profits and park the proceeds in money market funds. Remember, sell into strength when the opportunity presents itself. This principle also applies to any situation where it is becoming difficult to read the tea leaves, i.e. at transition stages, when you are not sure whether the pendulum is about to swing in the opposite direction. *When in doubt, sit it out!* Build up cash, sleep easier. Afraid of missing additional profits? Uh, uh. We are trying to win by not losing, not by staying at the party too long.

Conclusion: When conditions are normal, the majority of your assets will be in either stock or bond funds. When things are out of sync, use more cash.

Final warning: The purpose of the allocation examples above was merely to give you an idea about how to deal with active asset allocation. The numbers I used are neither absolutes nor ideals. As I have said so often, they are not chiseled in stone, but merely examples.

Your allocations will reflect you. Perhaps a bit more in money market funds than bond funds, less in conservative growth funds and more in equity income funds. Closer to the low ends of the bands in bearish times, higher to the upper ends of the bands in a bullish environment. Whatever, as long as it reflects you.

The point of moving targets in active asset allocation is to provide you with a discipline. As conditions change, your allocations must change. As the relative risk/reward parameters for the various assets classes in your portfolio shift, so must your mix. This is what staying on top of your portfolio is all about.

Benchmarks

"Okay," you're saying to yourself, "this is all fine and well. The idea of a finely structured portfolio spread across many different asset classes sounds great. To periodically fine-tune my holdings through active asset allocation makes a great deal of sense. I can see how this type of approach will keep me out of harm's way, protect me from my worst instincts. But there's a major problem here. I am a _____ (fill in the blank with any of the following, or choice of your own: doctor, schoolteacher, union official, retiree, corporate executive). I don't have the time, inclination, or training to make the type of decisions you are asking of me. How do I know when the economy is about to enter a recessionary phase, or interest rates are about to rise, or any of the other factors that impact on stock and bond prices? I'm not an economist."

Before you get completely frazzled, let me give you some good news: economists don't have the answers either. You see, the study of economics is one of the three professions (weather forecasting and security analysis being the other two) where you are paid a great deal of money to sound good, not necessarily to be right. (Put another way, how many winter days have you spent shoveling three inches of "partly cloudy" out of your driveway?) Anyone who has invested on the basis of pronouncements by the oft-quoted economic gurus in the financial press has generally gone broke very quickly.

So don't worry about your lack of time or professional

qualifications. You are *not* at a disadvantage. Recall that when we discussed manager selection (p. 39), I shared with you the insight that even full-time professional money managers do not have crystal balls. No one knows for certain what the future will bring. What we do is make educated guesses based on years of experience in the investment game. You don't have such experience? I am not here to blow sunshine in your face and attempt to convince you that within the confines of a couple of hundred pages I can make you the equal of a full-time professional.

What I *can* do is share with you some of the tricks of the trade to make the process attainable, regardless of your training or the time you have available. I call these "benchmarks." They are telltale signs that will guide you in making active asset allocation decisions. They will tell you when to add to your growth positions, when actually you might wish to pare back. They will show you when it might be more opportune to use bonds rather than stocks as a source of income.

I must warn you, however, that they are imprecise. Neither these benchmarks nor any other system, for that matter, can exactly pinpoint for you when stock prices have reached a high or a low. They cannot assure you that interest rates have bottomed and are about to reverse direction. No, they cannot do that. What they can do is show you when stock prices have entered a zone where they might be considered overvalued or undervalued. They can let you know when stock yields are more attractive than bond yields. But simply because stock prices are deemed to be overvalued, it does not mean they cannot become more overvalued; or conversely, if they are undervalued, they might become more undervalued.

That is why I prefer active asset allocation to market timing. We will begin paring back growth fund positions as equities become overvalued; we will add to bond fund positions as stock yields become even less attractive on a relative basis. In the first instance, if equities become even more overvalued, we will further reduce our growth fund holdings. That is what I mean by selling into strength and buying into weakness.

Only fools and those seeking to maximize gains believe it is possible to buy low and sell high. Realists, and those who wish to win by not losing, know that the road to success is to buy *lower* and sell *higher*.

So what are these benchmarks? What is this magic elixir? Plain and simple: they are a road map of market history (once again, "those who do not remember the past, will be condemned to repeat it"). Our thanks to the folks at The Leuthold Group (TLG) for their extremely fine work in this area. What TLG has done is track the market back to 1926 on a quarterly basis, looking at such factors as price/earnings ratios, stock and bond yields, price/book ratios, etc. This data has then been sorted into deciles. For instance, the 10 percent of the quarters during which the market traded at its lowest p/e ratios would constitute the bottom decile; the 10 percent of the quarters when the stocks market traded at its highest p/e ratios represent the highest decile. For the sake of discussion, we can say that based on the wealth of historical data, when the market is trading in the lowest three deciles it can be termed to be undervalued, in the middle four deciles fairly valued, and in the top three deciles overvalued.

Then we compute where the market is currently trading (this information can be easily acquired from a broker, financial section of a newspaper, or business magazines). If it falls within the bottom three deciles, you would want to begin adding to your growth positions. In the middle four deciles, maintain the status quo. In the top three deciles, begin paring back. Presto, benchmarks!

Let's look at some specific examples. Table 8.12 breaks out quarterly data on the price/earnings ratio for the S&P going back to 1926. Follow along with me: during

TABLE 8.12

S&P 500: P/E Ratios . . . Normalized

1926 to 3/31/91

This page presents a sideways histogram. The P/E buckets run along the bottom axis; the quarters (year-quarter) stack vertically above each bucket. The data is transcribed below with each P/E value and the quarters stacked above it (listed top → bottom as they appear in the figure).

P/E	Quarters (top → bottom)
5.0	32-2
5.5	—
6.0	—
6.5	33-1, 32-4, 32-3
7.0	32-1
7.5	—
8.0	82-3, 31-4
8.5	82-2, 82-1, 42-2
9.0	81-4, 42-3, 42-1, 33-2
9.5	81-3, 80-2, 53-3, 41-4
10.0	82-4, 80-1, 79-4, 79-3, 79-2, 79-1, 78-4, 78-1, 53-4, 53-2, 42-4, 41-2
10.5	83-1, 81-2, 81-1, 80-3, 78-2, 77-4, 74-4, 54-1, 53-1, 52-4, 52-3
11.0	52-2, 52-1, 51-4, 51-3, 51-2, 50-4, 51-1, 50-3, 50-1, 49-4, 43-1, 41-3
11.5	84-4, 83-4, 83-3, 83-2, 77-3, 75-1, 74-3, 54-2, 50-2, 43-4, 40-3, 33-3, 31-3
12.0	85-1, 77-2, 54-3, 44-3, 44-1, 43-3, 40-4, 40-2, 31-2
12.5	85-2, 77-1, 75-4, 75-3, 54-3, 44-2, 44-1, 43-2, 43-1, 34-3, 31-2
13.0	85-3, 76-4, 75-2, 57-4, 54-4, 48-1, 38-2, 34-2, 34-1, 30-4
13.5	85-4, 76-3, 76-2, 76-1, 58-1, 48-3, 45-1, 34-4, 31-1
14.0	70-3, 58-2, 55-1, 48-2, 40-1, 39-2, 35-1, 27-1, 26-4, 26-2
14.5	74-2, 70-2, 55-2, 47-4, 47-2, 45-2, 39-3, 38-1, 27-2, 26-3

"OUTLIERS" →

Distribution of P/E ratios (quarterly observations) with "OUTLIERS" extending to the right.

P/E	Observations (top → bottom)
15.0	86-1, 58-3, 57-3, 57-1, 47-3, 45-3, 39-4, 26-1
15.5	74-1, 70-1, 57-2, 47-1, 46-4, 39-1, 27-3
16.0	90-4, 88-4, 70-4, 56-4, 38-3, 37-4, 30-3, 28-1, 27-4
16.5	89-1, 88-2, 88-1, 86-4, 86-3, 86-2, 60-4, 58-4, 56-1, 55-4, 55-3, 45-4, 38-4, 35-2
17.0	90-3, 87-4, 73-4, 60-3, 60-2, 60-1, 59-2, 56-3, 56-2
17.5	91-1, 90-1, 89-2, 73-3, 71-4, 71-3, 71-1, 69-4, 69-3, 66-4, 62-3, 59-4, 59-3, 46-3, 46-1, 30-1, 28-3, 28-2
18.0	90-2, 89-4, 89-3, 73-2, 71-2, 68-1, 67-1, 66-3, 62-4, 59-1, 46-2, 30-2, 29-4
18.5	87-1, 72-1, 69-2, 68-3, 67-4, 66-... , 61-1
19.0	72-...
19.5	72-3, 72-2, 69-1, 68-3, 68-2, 67-4, 62-2, 35-3, 28-4
20.0	87-2, 73-1, 72-4, 68-4, 67-3, 67-2, 63-1, 61-2, 29-2
21.0	87-3, 66-2, 63-4, 63-3, 63-2, 61-3, 29-1
22.0	64-1, 62-1, 37-3, 35-4, 61-4, 29-1
23.0	66-1, 65-4, 65-3, 65-2, 65-1, 64-4, 64-3, 64-2, 37-3
24.0	29-3, 35-4
25.0	37-2
26.0	36-2, 36-1
27.0	
28.0	36-3
29.0	36-3, 36-4
30.0	37-1, 36-4

"OUTLIERS" →

Decile Distribution
(Excludes Outliers)

First Decile	Below 10.2
Second Decile	10.2 to 10.8
Third Decile	10.8 to 12.0
Fourth Decile	12.0 to 13.3
Fifth Decile	13.3 to 14.6
Sixth Decile	14.6 to 16.0
Seventh Decile	16.0 to 17.2
Eighth Decile	17.2 to 18.4
Ninth Decile	18.4 to 20.1
Tenth Decile	20.1 and above

First Decile–Third Decile } Stocks Cheap

Eighth Decile–Tenth Decile } Stocks Expensive

Median: 14.6
Average: 14.8

High Quartile: 17.7x earnings and above
Low Quartile: Below 11.3x earnings

Source: Copyright © 1991 by The Leuthold Group. Reprinted with permission.

the first quarter of 1986 (86-1) with the stock market trading at an average p/e of 14.5–15.0. By TLG's decile rankings, this put it in the sixth decile (fairly valued). For the balance of that year (86-2, 86-3, 86-4), its ratio stood at 16.0–16.5, or at the very upper limits of the fairly valued range. During 1987's first quarter (when a certain "wave theorist" was pictured on the cover of Barron's talking about the Dow Jones Average going straight to 3000–3500), this ratio had crept up to 18.5–19.0, or the ninth decile. *Warning bells! Sirens!* It was clearly time to begin reducing exposure to equity funds. You needed conviction, inner strength. Imagine the ribbing you were taking from friends for selling into this "greatest of all bull markets." Like laughter on the Titanic.

From March to June, the average p/e ratchets up again. Now it's at 19.5–20.0. *Close the hatches!* Time to reduce the percentages in growth funds again. Oh, the grief you are taking now. "You're selling out? Are you crazy? The world is awash in liquidity. There isn't enough stock to take care of the demand!" By the way, that last argument ranks right up there with tooth fairies, Santa Claus, and shares in the Brooklyn Bridge.

On to the fateful third quarter. Price/earnings ratios are now nearly off the top of the chart: 20.5–21.0. The bulls can hardly be reined in; the sky's the limit. *Dive, Dive, Dive!* By now your sell program should have been completed. So that when 12–19 October came along, you were already at the low exposure level others wished they were at.

Is this a form of "I told you so!"? No, it's a form of "History told you so!" Only those who subscribed to the notions that they did not wish to be confused by the facts, that their minds were already made up, were forced to wake up on 20 October and ask what hit them.

Please note too that no advanced degree in economics or investments was required to effectively execute this plan.

Let's look at this process from another vantage point. Table 8.13 plots average yields for the S&P 500 over the same period of time. Common sense would tell you that if stock prices are rising faster than dividends rates are being increased, such stocks are "rich" in price or overvalued. (A common method of assessing fair market values for equities is to employ a dividend discount model. This forecasts an expected stream of future dividends, discounted to present value, in order to determine a fair current price. The rationale is that a stock's price is linked to its ability to pay, and steadily increase, dividends. Growth in earnings facilitates dividend increases.)

Not to rub salt in the wound, but take note of the absurdly low yield to which the market had sunk by 1987's third quarter (87-3). It was literally a level never before seen; that's the epitome of the market being in uncharted waters!

The same active asset allocation techniques we utilized with the last chart are applicable here. Let's focus on another well-known turning point: 1982. Then, instead of the mass euphoria that prevailed in our previous example, we had virtually unbridled hysteria. Paul Volcker had arrived as Federal Reserve Board chairman in 1979, and by controlling money supply instead of rates, as had been the prior practice, created a series of sharp up and down spikes in the newly unlocked rates that totally unsettled Wall Street (and many would say unseated Jimmy Carter from the presidency). Doom and gloom spread throughout the investment markets, spurred on by an economic recession. What of yields? Check Table 8.14.

Get the idea? When they can't get rid of the stuff fast enough, when the customers tell their brokers "Sell at any price," buy it from them. Look how attractive a yield they attached to the stocks in order to induce you to be a buyer. When they can't buy enough of what's available, when all you need do is offer them a current yield of 3.0% (87-1), 2.9% (87-2), or better yet 2.8% (87-3) in order to get them to buy, sell it to them.

Move to the next table. Table 8.15 looks at another fea-

TABLE 8.13
S&P 500: Yields
1926 to 3/31/91

2.5	.6	.7	.8	.9	3.0	.2	.4	.6	.8	4.0	.2	.4	.6	.8	5.0	.2	.4	.6
			87-3	87-2	87-1	73-3	91-1	90-3	90-4	85-4	85-3	85-1	84-4	81-2	82-4	81-3	81-4	54-1
			73-1	72-1	73-2	71-4	90-2	89-2	88-3	76-4	85-2	84-1	84-3	81-1	80-3	80-1	80-2	52-4
			72-4	68-4	71-2	71-3	90-1	89-1	88-2	70-3	83-4	77-2	84-2	74-3	78-3	79-3	79-4	47-4
			72-3	64-3	69-2	71-1	89-4	88-4	76-2	70-2	83-3	57-4	83-1	54-3	77-4	79-2	78-1	43-1
			72-2	62-1	69-1	68-1	89-3	88-1	76-1	58-2	83-2	55-1	80-4	46-4	44-4	79-1	53-1	31-1
				61-4	68-3	67-2	86-4	87-4	74-2	57-1	77-1	45-3	77-3	45-1	44-3	78-4	48-3	
				61-3	68-2	66-2	86-3	86-1	57-3	55-2	75-4	45-2	75-1	39-2	43-3	78-2	38-3	
				61-2	67-4	63-4	86-2	76-3	57-2	46-3	75-3	34-2	54-4	37-2	43-2	74-4	33-2	
					67-3	63-3	73-4	74-1	56-4	38-4	75-2	28-1	47-1	35-2	39-4	54-2	26-1	
					66-1	63-2	69-4	70-4	56-3	36-2	58-1		39-3		39-1	48-2		
					65-4	63-1	69-3	70-1	56-2	34-1	39-1		33-4		37-3	47-3		
					65-3	61-1	67-1	66-4	56-1		37-1		30-3		34-3	47-2		
					65-2	59-4	62-2	66-3	55-4		36-4		27-4			44-2		
					65-1	59-2	60-2	62-4	55-3		36-3		27-3			44-1		
					64-4	59-1	60-1	62-3	46-1		35-3					43-4		
					64-2	29-3	58-4	60-4	45-4		33-3					40-1		
					64-1			60-3	36-1		30-2					35-1		
					59-3			58-3	35-4		29-4					27-1		
								58-1	28-4		28-3					26-4		
								46-2			28-2					26-3		
								29-2										
								29-1										

"OUTLIERS" →

	.8	6.0	.2	.4	.6	.8	7.0	.25	.50	.75	8.0	.25	.50	.75	9.0	9.5	10.0	11.0	12.0
	82-3																		
	82-2																		
	53-4																		
	53-3																		
	52-2																		
	52-1																		
	82-1	51-4																	
	53-2	48-4	42-4									42-2							
	52-3	48-1	40-4		51-3	50-1	51-1	51-2	42-3	50-4		42-1	32-3		32-1				32-2
	30-4	40-2	31-2	31-3	50-2	49-3	49-4	50-3	41-2	41-4									
	26-2				49-1	41-3	49-2	38-1	38-2										
					40-3	41-1	37-4	32-4	33-1										

Median: 4.23%
Average: 4.43%

High Quartile: 5.23% and above
Low Quartile: 3.51% and below

Stocks Cheap ⎫

Stocks Expensive ⎬

Decile Distribution
(Excludes Outliers)

First Decile . . . . 6.20% and above
Second Decile . . . . 6.20% to 5.43%
Third Decile . . . . 5.43% to 5.09%
Fourth Decile . . . . 5.09% to 4.64%
Fifth Decile . . . . 4.64% to 4.23%
Sixth Decile . . . . 4.23% to 3.89%
Seventh Decile . . . . 3.89% to 3.65%
Eighth Decile . . . . 3.65% to 3.36%
Ninth Decile . . . . 3.36% to 3.04%
Tenth Decile . . . . Below 3.04%

TABLE 8.14

Quarter	S&P Yield	Action
3rd Quarter, 1981	5.2%	Borderline undervalued; get ready
4th Quarter, 1981	5.4	Third decile; start buying
1st Quarter, 1982	5.8	Second decile; buy more
2nd/3rd Quarters, 1982	6.0	Second decile; fire sale, buy yet more

ture of stock valuation, price-to-book value. As a purchaser of a privately-held company must make a judgment as to how much of a premium, or multiple over book value, to pay, so must a buyer of shares in publicly-traded companies. Pay too large of a multiple, and it may take a great many years before your investment is rewarded. This, in fact, becomes evident when we study Table 8.15.

Is it any wonder that the Crash of '29 came with the market trading at an unmatched 4.0 price-to-book ratio (29-3)? Or that the market was equally deep into the tenth decile in the fall of 1987 (87-3) with a 2.6 ratio? Or just slightly behind at 2.3 at year-end 1989? Looking for bargains? How about buying stocks for exactly book value, which you could do in mid-1974 (1.0 in 74-3) and again in mid-1982 (1.0 in 82-3)! As I said, no advanced degrees required; just be a student of history.

Let's shift gears a little. Can the same techniques be used to assist in choosing between stocks and bonds as an alternative investment or as an alternative source of income? The answer is yes, but only to a limited degree. Check Table 8.16 which shows the ratios between yields on high-grade corporate bonds and the S&P 500. Since 1958, bonds have always yielded more than stocks, *ergo* a ratio of 1.0 or higher. The investor must have a truly long memory to recall that for a great part of the twentieth century, stocks (perceived as riskier investments) had to yield more than bonds ("risk free" investments that could be put away in a

vault, their coupons clipped twice yearly) to attract investors. Double-digit inflation, wide fluctuations in interest
rates, and large budget and trade deficits have put that
notion to rest. And from 1980 on, based on historical
deciles, stocks have never provided a preferred yield.
Throughout that time, the ratios have always ranked in the
highest three deciles.

On the surface, therefore, one should always look to
bonds as a source of income. But clearly this is not the
case. When interest rates are rising sharply, high-dividend-
paying stocks will most likely provide a much preferred
total rate of return. So as I said a moment ago, the information in this table can be useful, but only to a limited degree.

For instance: when the ratio reached an unheard of high
of 3.70-1 in 1987's third quarter, the die was clearly cast.
Bonds were evidently crying out as a safe haven. On the
other hand, as the great bull market of the 80s began in
1982's fourth quarter, the ratio at 2.40-1 was at the decade's
low end. (Not that bonds did poorly in the ensuing years.
As the effects of Volcker's anti-inflation campaign took
hold, interest rates came tumbling down. A carefully constructed bond portfolio from 1982–86 could have given an
investor a total return the equal of a stock portfolio.)

Such a ratio, therefore, must be dealt with carefully.
Perhaps in conjunction with absolute stock yields as de-
picted in Table 8.13, we can get a better handle on this
problematic situation. Note the first quarter of 1973, when
the great bear market of 1973–74 began: an all-time (at that
point) low yield in stocks—2.8%—coupled with an (until
then) all-time high bond-stock yield ratio—2.8–1 (Table
8.16). Ditto the third quarter of 1987: record low yield
coupled with a record high ratio. At the extremes, the figures never seem to lie.

Let's sum up. Benchmarks can prove a most useful tool
in undertaking active allocation. As stocks enter territory
where historically they have been proven to be overvalued,

TABLE 8.15
DJIA: Book Value Ratio
1926 to 3/31/91

.60	.70	.80	.90	1.00	1.05	1.10	1.15	1.20	1.25	1.30	1.35	1.40	1.45	1.50	1.55	1.60	1.65	1.70
32-2	33-1	74-4	82-2	82-3	81-2	75-4	82-4	77-1	84-2	84-4	85-1	85-3	57-4	85-4	72-4	62-2	66-4	63-3
		32-4	82-1	80-1	81-1	75-3	77-2	76-4	83-1	84-3	84-1	85-2	39-2	73-1	71-2	60-4	63-1	60-3
		32-3	81-4	79-4	80-4	75-2	74-2	76-1	76-3	73-4	83-3	83-4	37-4	72-3	69-3	55-1	58-3	57-2
			81-3	79-3	80-3	49-1	53-4	74-1	76-2	70-3	73-3	73-2		72-2	62-4	46-1	57-3	56-4
			80-2	79-2	77-3	48-4	53-3	54-1	52-2	70-2	70-4	71-4		72-1	45-4	38-3	57-1	35-4
			78-4	79-1	49-3	48-3	52-4	53-2	51-2	54-2	45-2	70-1		71-3	40-1		55-2	
			78-1	78-3	49-2	43-1	50-3	50-4	51-1	53-1	40-4	54-3		71-1	39-4		46-2	
			32-1	78-2	42-1	42-4	50-1	50-2	47-3	52-3	40-2	45-3		69-4	39-3		39-1	
				77-4		31-4	49-4	48-2	44-4	52-1	35-2	38-1		62-3	35-3		31-2	
				75-1			48-1	47-4	44-3	51-4				58-2				
				74-3			43-3	47-2	43-2	51-3				58-1				
				42-3			41-1	44-2	41-3	47-1				54-4				
				42-2			34-4	44-1		46-4				46-3				
				33-2			33-4	41-2		45-1				31-3				
							33-3	34-2		43-4								
										40-3								
										38-2								
										34-1								

1.75	1.80	1.85	1.90	1.95	2.00	2.10	2.20	2.30	2.40	2.50	2.60	2.70	2.90	3.00	3.25	3.50	3.75	4.00
						86-1												
					69-2	68-3												
				68-1	69-1	90-3												
66-3	68-2			88-3	91-1	90-1												
63-4	67-1	86-3		88-2	88-4	89-1	90-2											
63-2	62-1	68-4		88-1	87-4	66-1	89-2											
61-1	61-2	67-4	90-4	66-2	65-3	65-4	87-1											
60-2	60-1	67-2	86-4	64-3	64-2	65-2	37-1											
56-1	58-4	64-1	86-2	59-3	37-3	65-1	27-2	89-4										
55-4	56-3	61-4	67-3	59-2	37-2	64-4	26-3	89-3	30-3				30-2					
55-3	56-2	61-3	59-4	36-3	30-4	27-1	26-1	87-2	28-1		87-3		30-1			29-2		
38-4	36-1	36-2	59-1	31-1	26-2	26-4		27-3	27-4		28-2	28-3	29-4		28-4	29-1		29-3

Decile Distribution

First Decile	Below 1.01
Second Decile	1.01 to 1.16
Third Decile	1.16 to 1.23
Fourth Decile	1.23 to 1.31
Fifth Decile	1.31 to 1.43
Sixth Decile	1.43 to 1.57
Seventh Decile	1.57 to 1.74
Eighth Decile	1.74 to 1.87
Ninth Decile	1.87 to 2.09
Tenth Decile	2.09 and above

Stocks Undervalued

Stocks Overvalued

Average: 1.54
Median: 1.43

High Quartile: 1.30 and above
Low Quartile: 1.20 and below

TABLE 8.16
The Yield Ratio
Bond Yields/Stock Yields
1957 to 3/31/91

.90	1.00	1.10	1.20	1.30	1.40	1.50	1.60	1.70	1.80	1.90	2.00	2.10	2.20
						65-3							
						65-2							
					63-4	65-1	78-1	77-4					
					63-3	64-4	65-4	67-1	79-2				
			62-4		63-2	64-3	61-4	66-4	79-1				
			62-3	63-1	61-1	64-2	61-3	66-3	78-4	79-3	77-1	79-4	80-2
58-2			58-3	62-2	60-4	64-1	61-2	66-2	78-3	77-2	75-1	76-4	70-3
			57-3	60-3	60-2	62-1	59-3	66-1	78-2	74-4	68-1	74-3	68-3
58-1	57-4	57-1	57-2	58-4	59-1	60-1	59-2	59-4	77-3	67-2	67-3		67-4
.90	1.00	1.10	1.20	1.30	1.40	1.50	1.60	1.70	1.80	1.90	2.00	2.10	2.20

2.30	2.40	2.50	2.60	2.70	2.80	2.90	3.00	3.10	3.20	3.30	3.40	3.50	3.60	3.70
				91-1										
				90-3										
				89-4										
				88-4	90-2									
	82-4		88-2	88-3	90-1									
	76-2		88-1	86-3	89-3									
	76-1		86-4	86-2	89-2									
	74-2	90-4	83-1	86-1	89-1		84-3							
	73-4		82-3	82-2	83-2	87-1	84-2							
	76-3	71-4	80-3	82-1	85-4		83-4							
	75-4	71-1	80-1	73-2	85-3		83-3							
	75-3	70-4	73-3	72-4	85-2	87-4	81-4							
	75-2	70-1	72-1	72-3	84-4	85-1	81-1							
	74-1	69-3	71-3	72-2					91-3					
	68-2	68-4	69-2	71-2	69-4	73-1	84-1	80-4	91-2	87-2				87-3
2.30	**2.40**	**2.50**	**2.60**	**2.70**	**2.80**	**2.90**	**3.00**	**3.10**	**3.20**	**3.30**	**3.40**	**3.50**	**3.60**	**3.70**

Stocks Cheap   }   91-3, 91-2

Stocks Expensive   }

Average: 2.20%
Median: 2.30%

Low Quartile: 1.61 and below
High Quartile: 2.67 and above

Decile Distribution

First Decile	1.36 and below
Second Decile	1.36 to 1.52
Third Decile	1.52 to 1.71
Fourth Decile	1.71 to 1.96
Fifth Decile	1.96 to 2.30
Sixth Decile	2.30 to 2.46
Seventh Decile	2.46 to 2.61
Eighth Decile	2.61 to 2.72
Ninth Decile	2.72 to 2.84
Tenth Decile	2.84 and above

start scaling back. As they enter an undervalued zone, begin buying. Remember, we are trying to phase in and phase out, not buy at the low (there might be a lower low) and sell at the high (there might be a higher high). That's the difference between active asset allocation and market timing. *Sell into strength and buy into weakness.* And let the benchmarks be your guide.

MUTUAL FUND SELECTION

So now we have reached the last step. We have established our objective, our goal. Accordingly, we established an asset/section allocation to reflect our objective and our perception of where we currently stood in terms of stock and bond valuations (benchmarks, bands, and targets). Finally, we must flesh out this framework with a selection of tortoise funds to complete the portfolio.

Keep in mind our goal: *to build in as much diversification as possible.* The more diversification, the less likelihood of a major disaster (always remember a loss of 50 percent requires double that as a gain—100 percent—simply to break even). So in selecting funds to fill in the grid, we want to ensure that they will maximize asset class and manager diversification in the most efficient way possible. There is, of course, the potential of overdiversification, but if we follow the guidelines provided in Chapter 6, we can create a fully diversified portfolio and yet retain efficiency. Perhaps "fully diversified but manageable" is the equivalent of "having your cake and eating it too."

The question, then, is how many funds comprise a fully diversified portfolio? Unfortunately, there is no set answer. There is no magic number. All I can say is that in recent years, with turbulence in the marketplace and the variety of financial instruments exploding, I have found myself utilizing an ever larger number of funds (safety in numbers). Ten years ago, I had client portfolios with as few as ten funds. Five years ago, the number had grown to fifteen. Today, I am not truly comfortable with less than twenty. Admittedly more work, but the times demand it. How else to survive the roller coaster ride?

Danger: On this very point, I have often been asked the following: If a typical portfolio consists of five sectors (aggressive growth, conservative growth, equity income, fixed income, and money market), is it not sufficient to simply purchase one fund per sector, for a five-fund multifund portfolio? My answer remains the same—it's better than owning but a single fund, but the strategy is full of holes and will likely fail to perform up to expectations in a given market environment.

If you recall our discussion on style diversification (pp. 94–101), you know what these holes are. Assume, for instance, the fund you select for aggressive growth specializes in small-cap stocks. Assume that aggressive growth represents 20 percent of your total assets. What happens during those periods of time (normally five out of every ten years) when small-cap stocks underperform high-cap stocks? Right. Twenty percent of your portfolio will drag down total performance for half of each decade!

Instead, what if you owned five aggressive growth funds of which only one specializes in small-cap stocks? Under the same assumptions, only 4% of your portfolio (20% ÷ 5) would be predestined to lag the averages while such stocks are out of favor. I cannot stress it enough: *concentration sows the seeds of potential disaster!* One style per sector is *not* diversification! You might have numerical diversification and minimal asset class diversification, but you don't have manager diversification, except in the most simplistic, unacceptable sense.

Danger: Now let's examine the other side of the coin: how many funds are too many to own? True, there is safety in numbers, but there comes a time when literally "too

much of a good thing" is no good. In mutual fund portfolios it comes when you have too much overlap.

In selecting tortoise funds, we looked to process (style)
as the third qualification. We want each fund in our portfolio to have an investment style that complements the
others. There is very little to be gained by having two or
three managers selecting high-grade, long-term corporate
bonds; three or four selecting which emerging growth
stocks we should own; and two or three selecting high-
dividend-paying stocks. If you have too many managers
playing on the same field, it becomes more and more likely
that they will cancel each other out (one buying a certain
stock or bond while the other sells it).

How to prevent this? The overlap test (p. 99). You may
think each manager you wish to add to your portfolio
brings a new perspective to the selection process, but how
true is this? Test for overlap. Assume you currently own
five aggressive growth funds and want to add a sixth. Put
together a list of the top ten holdings of the five funds you
currently own and compare the top ten holdings of the
candidate. Does adding the sixth enhance diversification,
or do you simply end up owning more of the same stocks
(overlap)? There are no hard and fast rules, but if adding
a new fund creates overlap exceeding 20–25 percent, then
the benefits of further diversification are suspect.

So too should you periodically test for overlap in your
current list of fund holdings (perhaps quarterly). If the
investment styles of your various managers begin to drift
ever closer together, evidenced by their owning more and
more of the same stocks and bonds, perhaps it's time for
some alterations to the manager lineup! Investing is not a
static process. Because a manager was doing one thing in
March, you cannot assume he or she is doing the exact
same thing in June. (In the next chapter we shall look
into the constant monitoring a multifund portfolio requires).

Warning: The day you start believing you know in advance which fund, or more precisely which investment style, will outperform in the period ahead, is the day you start heading down the road to failure. In other words, *don't show favoritism among funds in a single sector!*

You have identified five conservative growth funds that you are comfortable owning in your portfolio. Your research leads you to believe they have complementary investment styles. Your asset/sector allocation at present calls for 25 percent of the portfolio to be invested in such funds. Result: invest 5 percent in each of these five funds. Remember, we are trying to protect the downside, not maximize the upside. Overweighing one or two of these five in the belief they may outperform in the year ahead could conceivably enhance returns if in fact they outperform. But what if you guess wrong? Then you have potentially crippled your downside protection.

Trust in your overall selection process. If you properly applied the "Three P's" in picking tortoise funds for your portfolio, then as long as the majority of them, 1 percent better than 50 percent, perform up to expectations and up to their past record of delivering consistent, above-average returns, then your portfolio will always achieve its desired objective of winning by not losing. Don't make bets! Excitement and gambling are for the casinos. Safe, consistent, risk-averse returns are what you are trying to achieve, and you will if you rely on the inherent strengths of a tortoise fund portfolio that is evenly weighted within sectors.

Let's recap:

1. In mutual fund selection, our goal is to maximize numerical, asset class, and manager diversification.

2. There is no perfect number of funds that is exactly right for your portfolio.

3. One fund per sector provides numerical diversification and a degree of asset class diversification, but totally insufficient style diversification.

4. Owning too many funds, as determined primarily by applying our overlap test, will increase costs with no incremental benefit.

5. Within sectors, equally weight your allocation to each fund. You do not improve your chances of reducing downside risks by playing favorites.

With those ground rules in place, let's now put together a true tortoise multifund portfolio. I must admit at the very outset that I do so with some trepidation. I am putting this portfolio together in early 1991; publicly available copies of this book will be available later this year. Hopefully, there will be some who are reading this section for the first time two, three, four, or five years thereafter. So, you the reader, please understand: some of what you are reading might be outdated as you read it. Why? A portfolio manager might have left. An investment style may be altered. A fund manager might have lost the touch. Or most simply, another fund with a similar style and a preferred overall complexion has been identified. So take what you are about to read with a grain of salt.

It is provided as an example, to show you how a defensive, totally diversified portfolio is put together. The particulars are not as important as the overall construction. If you learn the procedure, the rest will fall into place. As they attempt to teach in business school: *Don't get hung up on details!* In this case, the big picture is more important than the parts. The parts are detailed here for the sake of example alone.

Having said that, let's get to work. To steer you through the process, I am going to put together a portfolio with a balanced objective, the mid-point of the five major types of objectives set out for you on pages 119–124, while the neutral mode is the mid-point of the five moving targets described on pages 142–154. This will, therefore, be the widest ranging portfolio possible in terms of breadth and types of components, and as a result, will be the most instructive of the process.

SAMPLE PORTFOLIO*

OBJECTIVE: BALANCED   ENVIRONMENT: NEUTRAL

Asset/Sector Allocation

Aggressive Growth	15%	*Conservative Growth*	20%
AIM Weingarten	3%	AIM Charter	4%
FPA Paramount	3	Gabelli Asset	4
Janus Venture	3	Gabelli Growth	4
N.Y. Venture	3	Invest. Co. Amer.	4
WPG Tudor	3	Phoenix Growth	4

Equity Income	25%	*Fixed Income*	30%
Frankl. Mgd. Ris. Div.	5%	Bernst. Int. Dur.	6%
Financial Industrial	5	Frankl. U.S. Govt.	6
Putnam G. & I.	5	MFS Bond	6
Wash. Mut. Inv.	5	PIMIT Tot. Ret.	6
Wellington Fund	5	Vanguard F.I. Treas.	6

*Data as of 31 December 1990

Aggressive Growth

1. *AIM Weingarten*

   Assets: $597 million 3-Yr. Avg. Annual Return: 16.9%
   Portfolio Manager (First Year): Harry Hutzler (1983)
   Style: 50% established growth companies, 50% earnings surprises.

2. *FPA Paramount*

   Assets: $199 million 3-Yr. Avg. Annual Return: 14.2%
   Portfolio Manager (First Year): William Sams (1981)
   Style: Value driven, 70% in established companies with
   favorable earnings outlook, 30% special situations (initial public offerings, small-caps). Up to 50% cash.

3. *Janus Venture*

   Assets: $224 million 3-Yr. Avg. Annual Return: 18.2%
   Portfolio Manager (First Year): Jim Craig (1985)
   Style: Emerging growth stocks. Top–down approach
   (from themes to individual issues).

4. *N.Y. Venture*

   Assets: $286 million 3-Yr. Avg. Annual Return: 16.4%
   Portfolio Manager (First Year): Shelby Davis (1969)
   Style: Solid growth companies at relatively low multi-
   ples in industries selected to benefit from pre-identified
   trends.

5. *WPG Tudor*

   Assets: $171 million 3-Yr. Avg. Annual Return: 11.4%
   Portfolio Manager (First Year): Melville (Mickey)
   Strauss (1973)
   Style: 50% emerging growth companies, 50% special
   situations; will use hedging techniques.

Conservative Growth

1. *AIM Charter*

   Assets: $99 million   3-Yr. Avg. Annual Return: 15.7%
   Portfolio Manager (First Year): Julian Lerner (1968)
   Style: Companies undergoing earnings' acceleration.
   Well-known companies with good management.

2. *Gabelli Asset*

   Assets: $327 million 3-Yr. Avg. Annual Return: 15.7%
   Portfolio Manager (First Year): Mario Gabelli (1986)

Style: Bottom-up approach, selection based on private market valuations. Cash allowed to build up when no such values are available.

3. *Gabelli Growth*

Assets: $185 million 3-Yr. Avg. Annual Return: 23.9%
Portfolio Manager (First Year): Elizabeth Bramwell (1987)
Style: Top–down to industry selection. Earnings growth for individual issues. Bias towards "Manufacturing America."

4. *Investment Co. of America*

Assets: $5.3 Billion   3-Yr. Avg. Annual Return: 13.8%
Portfolio Manager (First Year): William Newton (team approach)
Style: Conservative, value approach. Large-cap bias with buy and hold strategy.

5. *Phoenix Growth*

Assets: $681 million 3-Yr. Avg. Annual Return: 13.8%
Portfolio Manager (First Year): Robert Chesek (1980)
Style: Stocks selected on the basis of earnings momentum, growth rates, and value.

Equity Income

1. *Franklin Managed Rising Dividend*

Assets: $35 million   3-Yr. Avg. Annual Return: 12.9%
Portfolio Manager (First Year): William Lippman (1960), with predecessor funds.
Style: Stocks displaying consistent dividend growth, strong balance sheets, selling in lower half of p/e range.

2. *Financial Industrial Income*

Assets: $483 million 3-Yr. Avg. Annual Return: 15.4%
Portfolio Manager (First Year): John J. Kaweske (1985)

Style: Top–down macroeconomic analysis, bottom-up fundamental analysis, thematic selection (e.g., health care).

3. *Putnam Growth & Income*

Assets: $1.9 billion   3-Yr. Avg. Annual Return: 14.3%
Portfolio Manager (First Year): John Maurice (1968)
Style: Primarily in stocks, some bonds to boost yield. Favors stocks with high yields, earnings growth, and low p/e and price-to-book ratios.

4. *Washington Mutual Investors*

Assets: $4.9 billion   3-Yr. Avg. Annual Return: 11.0%
Portfolio Manager (First Year): James Dunton/Stephen Bepler (team approach)
Style: Undervalued, top-quality companies with long dividend history. Usually stays fully invested.

5. *Wellington Fund*

Assets: $2.2 billion   3-Yr. Avg. Annual Return: 12.2%
Portfolio Manager (First Year): Vincent Bajakian (1979)
Style: Balanced approach (usually 60% stocks, 40% bonds). Emphasis on conservatively valued, large-cap issues with high current income; high-grade corporate bonds.

Fixed Income

1. *Bernstein Intermediate Duration*

Assets: $243 million   3-Yr. Avg. Annual Return: N/A
Portfolio Manager (First Year): David Levine, Elizabeth Ruskin, Frances Trainer (team approach)
Style: Duration varies ± 1 year around Shearson Lehman Government/Corporate Index. Flexible in terms of sectors and quality (usually high). Identify security

and sector mispricing, anticipate interest rates, and exploit yield curve distortions.

2. *Franklin U.S. Government*

Assets: $11.4 billion 3-Yr. Avg. Annual Return: 10.3%
Portfolio Manager (First Year): Jack Lemein (1984)
Style: Concentrates on GNMA's. Dominant position in marketplace due to size. Balances portfolios by coupons, pools, maturities.

3. *MFS Bond*

Assets: $287 million 3-Yr. Avg. Annual Return: 9.6%
Portfolio Manager (First Year): Patricia Zlotin (lead manager)
Style: Opportunistic. Interest rate anticipation, will use foreign bonds, municipal bonds. Active swapping. In-house credit research.

4. *PIMIT Total Return*

Assets: $851 million 3-Yr. Avg. Annual Return: 10.5%
Portfolio Manager (First Year): William H. Gross (1987)
Style: Duration ± 1.5 years around Shearson Lehman G/C index. Flexible and quite aggressive in terms of sector selections—utilizes proprietary computer models. Interest rate anticipation based on long-term secular forecast.

5. *Vanguard Fixed Income Treasuries*

Assets: $537 million 3-Yr. Avg. Annual Return: 10.9%
Portfolio Manager (First Year): Tony Jiorle (1988)
Style: Tracks the Shearson Lehman Long Term Treasury Index, ± ½ year. Seeks inefficiencies in bond pricing to add value.

That's it! Here is your fully developed portfolio of tortoise funds. It displays tremendous numerical diversification and asset class mix—and a team of managers that would be the envy of even the most well-entrenched pension officer of a Fortune 500 company. There are, of course, many other good tortoise managers who make it through the screening process, but as I said earlier, this group is quite representative of them all.

Look at this lineup. Can you conceive of any market/ economic environment in which these managers would leave you exposed to market-topping losses? I can't, perhaps with the exception of a total cataclysm in the developed world's financial structure. These and the twenty or so others who make it through the screens are the "top guns" of the investing world. Would you rather (1) pick stocks and bonds by yourself, (2) follow the advice of a broker or friend, (3) hand over your portfolio to a single portfolio manager, or (4) implement the tortoise fund portfolio approach? My vote is with (4).

Now I hope you understand why I said earlier that this approach lets you sleep well at night. When you have such a team of quality specialists investing on your behalf each and every day, you need not worry what might be awaiting you around the next bend. Will they all perform well every year? No, but that's almost immaterial, as long as you have structured your asset/sector allocation properly, and as long as you have been thorough in your mutual fund selections. Then even if a few of these "stars" underperform each year, you will not care. Your portfolio will still go plodding along. Reasonable returns in up markets, far-above-average returns in down markets.

Will some of them underperform each year? Sure. They're human, remember. The 95 percent of funds that don't make it into your portfolio might underperform one out of two years. These tortoises will have one bad year in four, or one in five (even one in three occasionally). No one is perfect! So if you have a portfolio of twenty tortoises, four or five are sure to be having a subpar year, but you don't care because the other fifteen or sixteen will be doing their thing.

If you're looking to outperform in up markets, this is not the way. Too many plodders, some resting each year. Too much diversification, too many individual stocks, too many industry groups, too many different fund managers with ideas of their own. *But if you're looking to stay out of hot water, there's no better way. This is an unbeatable team!*

9

KEEPING THE PORTFOLIO FRESH

HOW CONVENIENT it would be if one could go through this process but once, build a bullet-proof portfolio and put it away. Convenient, yes, but totally unrealistic. I have stressed many times throughout the course of this book that "buy and hold," "safe havens," "blue chips," and other such notions simply will not work in today's fast paced, rapidly changing investment world.

Factors which have an impact on the various aspects of our type of portfolio—objective, asset/sector allocation, fund selection—require periodic review. Nothing is chiseled in stone. What was applicable a year ago, a month ago, even a week ago, may no longer be so. Change is what the investment world is all about.

In Chapter 7, we looked at the time involved in the four types of asset allocation. Clearly, there is a time factor here as well. Portfolio maintenance requires time. The more time you have available, the better. You've sown the seeds in your garden, and now you must cultivate them. Watering, hoeing, pruning, weeding—all are important in maintaining the quality of your initial work.

So it is with portfolios. After your initial construction work, you must perform periodic "gardening" tasks to maintain the health of your portfolio—checking objectives, monitoring changes in the investment climate which may affect asset and sector allocation, reviewing the Three P's of fund selection. All must be performed with some degree of regularity if your portfolio is to stay in tune with the times.

How often? That will depend on you, the individual. I cannot prescribe with exactitude, because each of your situations is different. A car manufacturer might tell you to change your oil every 3,000 miles; your lifestyle and schedule might only allow you to do it every 3,500 miles. So let me provide you with a Manufacturer's Suggested Maintenance Schedule for your portfolio. Your individual circumstances will determine how closely you stick to it.

The maintenance schedule parallels the building process. Three areas must be reviewed: objective, asset/sector allocation, and fund selection. Let's look at the maintenance process for each.

OBJECTIVE

Frankly, if you spent sufficient time pinpointing your objective to begin with, maintenance will neither be time consuming nor occur often. Did you truly apply the principle of "Know thyself?" Did you truly gauge how ironclad your stomach was?

The better the job you did in originally fixing your objective, the easier it will be to maintain it. But no doubt about it—however well you initially performed objective setting, you must check it nonetheless. How often?

I believe an annual checkup is in order. Bring your financial picture up to date. Consider your savings accounts, income from earnings and other sources, budget, years left to retirement, etc. Are the financial assumptions upon which you based your objectives still valid? Is your portfolio still generating sufficient income to allow you to maintain your lifestyle?

Perhaps there was a large drop in interest rates over the past twelve months. The amount of current income being generated by your portfolio with an income objective no longer is meeting your needs A shift to a maximum yield objective might be called for.

The child for whose college education expenses you were investing is finally graduating. Yet you are still ten to fifteen years away from retiring. Maybe more growth can be built into the portfolio by changing from a balanced objective to growth.

Or the day for which you planned so long has finally arrived—you retire. After juggling all the numbers, it appears you will need the income generated by your portfolio to supplement other sources. Switch from balanced to income.

Notice, please, that the situations we are citing here do not occur that frequently. Also note that I have not cited a single instance of market events triggering a change in objective. Why? Because they shouldn't! If you didn't prepare properly, reactive objective setting will start you on the road to calamity.

October 1987. The stock market sinks 30 percent in six days. "I don't think the stock market is for me. I'll shift my objective more towards income." 1988–89. The loss is made up; stocks up over 30 percent in 1989 alone. "Well, I guess I should have stayed. Let's shift towards growth." Etc., etc., etc. Don't treat yourself like a yo-yo. It can't lead to any good.

Movements in the stock and bond markets should trigger changes in asset/sector allocation, *not* in objective.

ASSET/SECTOR ALLOCATION

Remember our discussion on moving targets on page 142? That's the essence of maintenance. Because I am a full-time portfolio manager, this is a daily process for me. Particularly with the current pace of events, you cannot let too much water flow under the bridge before making adjustments. Example: you are negative on stocks due to a belief that the recession is deepening. Suddenly, back-to-back economic reports (e.g., corporate earnings and plant utilization) show flat or higher quarter to quarter comparisons.

Time to adjust. You obviously misread the tea leaves. It may not yet be a trend, but it's better to be early than late, and you're not going to be making a drastic shift—no more than 5–10 percent. Continue to track ongoing developments in order to confirm or contradict earlier reports. In any case, warning bells should begin ringing in your head.

Consult the price/earnings, price/book, price/yield charts. Is the trend still heading in the same direction or has it reversed? (Note: a stall is not a cause of alarm. Look at the charts on pages 158–169. Quite often in the past you will see instances where a trend developed in a certain direction and then held in a specific decile for a number of quarters. In these cases it is not necessarily better to be early. Wait for a reversal, not a halt.)

What maintenance schedule should non-professionals use for asset/sector allocation review? I would say no less than quarterly. But, this is not cast in stone. Let events call the shots. You last reviewed your asset/sector allocations on 30 September 1987 and had correctly built up cash and fixed-income in your mix. Along comes the October crash. The time to begin redeploying into stocks is 20 October, not at your next scheduled review post-31 December. To stick with our auto analogy, when you hear a loud clanking noise in your engine, you take the car in immediately; you don't wait for your next scheduled checkup.

This schedule presumes you are using the preferred method of allocation: active asset allocation. If, instead, you are more comfortable with fixed mix, reviews will occur with much less frequency. On the other hand, if you are a believer in market timing, reviews will occur with much greater regularity.

Remember that this is a check-up. Your portfolio/auto might be running perfectly. Don't fool yourself into believing you must do something simply because three months have passed and nothing has been done to reshape or fine-tune your portfolio. If your previous readings of the economic/market environment were correct and you therefore properly structured your portfolio, no action might be necessary for some time. For my own client portfolios, I have gone from twelve to fifteen months without adjusting allocations. Sometimes events unfold rapidly; sometimes they don't.

Go with the flow.

FUND SELECTION

The tests used to select funds in the first place—consistent performance, people, process—are the tests applied for periodic maintenance. Has the performance continued as expected? Are the same people still at the helm? Is the same investment process still being applied in a disciplined fashion? Let's look at these one by one.

Performance:

As I said earlier, even tortoises will occasionally pause for a rest. A quarter, six months, or a year in the 50th to 60th percentile is to be expected. It can go on longer—if a manager's area of expertise is out of favor in the market for extended periods (e.g. small cap or basic value), only a truly exceptional talent will be able to overcome such a hurdle. That is why it is important to measure your managers against their peers as well. If a small-cap fund has stayed below the 50th percentile in the fund universe for over a year, take a look at how other small-cap managers performed over the same period of time.

How about a lengthy fall into the 80th to 99th percentiles? Something is definitely wrong! You had better quickly reexamine all your assumptions. Very likely you missed some critical element such as assuming the fund was run by committee when it really was run on a star system. Or one of the other two P's has changed—a new manager or a new investment process has been put into place.

Warning: Don't be trigger happy. I repeat, even tortoises rest. There are no all-weather managers. However few or many funds in your portfolio, they will not be all performing well all the time. If you own ten tortoises, expect two to three to rest each year. As long as the majority are delivering, there is nothing to be concerned about.

People

As I said on page 88, if you own a fund run by a star, take great care that that individual remains at the helm. People run funds. Maintenance, therefore, involves checking this critical aspect. In a committee system, change has a less drastic effect, unless there was a mass exodus (it doesn't hurt to ask the question even if the possibilities of such an event are rather slim).

What if, in fact, the star has left? Don't get alarmed. Simply rev up the research engine—who is the successor? What is this person's background? Was he groomed by the star? Does he intend to leave the star's portfolio policy in place or to recast it in his own image?

Whatever the answers, there is no rush. Few new managers are given carte blanche to make wholesale liquidations in the existing portfolio, particularly if the star had been delivering satisfactory performance ("If it ain't broke, don't fix it"). However, this assumes the star left of his or her own volition; be sure to check. Otherwise, follow the fund for the ensuing one to three quarters to see if the successor is able to fill the star's shoes.

If performance begins to tail off (unrelated to a weaker market or a style falling out of favor—check the peer group), it's time to part company. In the time since you became aware of the star's departure, some alternate tortoise funds will probably have made it through your screens. Transfer the proceeds into these new funds.

Process

You hope the managers have stuck to their knitting. You hope they know not to fix that which is not broken—unless there was no discipline to speak of in the first place. That is what you will discover through these checkups.

If there is a change in process, why? Simply a hair-trigger reaction to the previous style falling temporarily out of favor? Shooting from the hip? Panic? So many of the critical features of our portfolio depend on each manager sticking to his or her style that any deviations from form deserve immediate attention. Go back to our football analogy: if your left tackle suddenly begins playing like a right guard, what happens to your team? Line play breaks down and brings your entire offense to its knees.

A review of the most recent semi-annual or annual report or a call to the fund group will yield the required information. Same policy in place? Unusual level of sales and purchases of portfolio positions? If a fund's policy was to always keep its yield above the market's, what explains a sudden drop below the market's? A bond fund whose portfolio has been concentrated in investment grade issues suddenly takes a 25 percent position in junk bonds. Why? A balanced fund whose style was to limit bond holdings to no more than 25 percent of total assets now has 40 percent in fixed income instruments. Explanation?

With performance, I warned you not to be trigger happy. With style/process the opposite is true. Discipline means the slightest of variations is suspect. You want your fund managers to stick precisely to their knitting. Any stray motion must be questioned. Otherwise, subsequent "surprises" can be quite harsh.

How often should you check on your fund selections? My gut tells me no less than monthly, but I realize that with many readers' busy lifestyles this may not be possible. In that case, I would say no less than once a quarter. The sooner you are aware of a problem, the sooner you are able to identify it and correct it.

SUMMARY—MAINTENANCE SCHEDULE

1. Objective: Annually.
2. Asset/Sector Allocation: As events warrant, but not less than quarterly.
3. Fund Selection: Preferably monthly, but not less than quarterly.

CODA

WE ARE through; we have filled in all the gaps. We know now why we win by not losing, and we know how:

1. We must be invested to achieve long-term goals; savings vehicles are suitable only for savings purposes, not investment.
2. All investments have risk.
3. Risk is multifaceted: inflation, liquidity, numerical, etc.
4. The greatest risk of all is the risk of losses.
5. Losses have a greater impact on long-term performance than do gains (the 20/20 trap).
6. Large losses require much larger gains to offset them ($-50\% + 100\% =$ break even).
7. The way to reduce risk is to diversify.
8. The way to reduce the risk of major losses is to maximize diversification.

9. The most efficient way to maximize diversification is to hold a portfolio of mutual funds.

10. Our preference among funds is that very small subset that we call tortoise funds.

11. The way to identify tortoise funds is via "The Three P's": Performance (consistent), People (well-entrenched managers assisted by sufficient internal research and analysis), and Process (a disciplined, well-defined investment style).

12. A three-step, portfolio-building approach: objective setting, asset/sector allocation, and fund selection.

13. Check the portfolio periodically to keep it fresh. Objective: annually. Asset/sector allocation: at least quarterly. Fund selection: preferably monthly, but not less than quarterly.

That is how you win by not losing. That is the way to achieve your goals and sleep easy along the way.

Good luck!

POSTSCRIPT

THROUGHOUT THIS book, I have pointed out how rapidly events are unfolding in the current investment environment. Little did I realize that a number of issues I have raised would already be coming to fruition before the text even went to print. To wit:

GUARANTEES

As the reader will recall, I have gone to some lengths to rid investors of the notion that any investment is truly guaranteed. Two developments: One, government regulators recently opined that no mutual fund product should carry the word "guarantee" in its name. Even if the fund is invested solely in U.S. Treasury Bonds ("principal guaranteed by the U.S. Government"), that supposed guarantee applies only to the underlying bonds, not to the principal of the fund itself. Since fund assets are "marked to the market" each day, investors are sure to suffer loss of principal, particularly if interest rates are rising.

Second, and much more heart rending, millions of dollars—correction, hundreds of millions of dollars—in losses are now being suffered by investors who innocently bought into "guaranteed investment contracts" (a.k.a. "GIC's" or "gicks").

As I said on page 14, a guaranteed investment is a contradiction in terms. When that guarantee is supplied by an insurance company which subsequently goes bust, like First Executive and all the others which are sure to follow, it literally is not worth the paper it is written on.

INTERNATIONAL

On page 44 under "Many Faces of Risk," I listed "International." I'm sure this raised some eyebrows, particularly among those who bought the party line about how much sense it made to diversify on an international scale.

With the unfolding developments in Tokyo, where it has now been revealed that favored clients—so far, including one industrial giant—are paid back for losses suffered in declining markets, foreign investors have a new element of risk to contend with: the foreign dealer may be dealing to his friends from the bottom of the deck. Care to take a seat, sucker?

July 6, 1991

INDEX